"*Owning Our Struggles* is a book that fills in so many of the gaps often present in traditional self-help books, which tend to over-emphasize the importance of 'the self' in healing, and under-estimate the importance of community and culture. Written through the lens of deep expertise, lived experience, and sincere compassion, it reminds us that healing does not happen in individual silos. And that wholeness comes when we own our brokenness—especially the parts of ourselves that dominant culture has taught us to believe are broken. Through storytelling, reflections, and practical exercises, Minaa B. teaches us how to own our struggles—so that our struggles no longer own us."

—Layla F. Saad, *New York Times* bestselling author of *Me and White Supremacy*

"Minaa's writing is a gift to us all. She gracefully and compassionately invites every reader to acknowledge and face confronting truths about a broken system that we live in, contribute to, and for many, often deny. In her debut book, Minaa generously shares her own story, the stories of others, as well as research to make a powerful case for a path forward for BIPOC individuals to heal pain and trauma. Community care is the answer. And as Minaa suggests, the ways we connect with one another and care for one another in our communities is the catalyst for the change we seek. This book is for every human because healing happens when we have a community upon which we can count. We don't arrive alone; we arrive with others."

—Vienna Pharaon, LMFT, national bestselling author of *The Origins of You*

"This book is a treasure. A collaborative tool for your healing journey. Minaa effortlessly weaves personal stories with deep research and hands-on exercises that feel like a bright light in a dark world. There is space, care, and a feeling of love for us to be free from trauma in the pages. A book to read slowly with a journal and pen."

—Tricia Hersey, founder of the Nap Ministry and author of
Rest Is Resistance: A Manifesto

"When I read Minaa B.'s book, my first thought was 'She truly gets it!' She sees the importance of relationships and how we think, feel, and choose, and how this can impact how we function in our day-to-day lives and our ability to overcome traumas through community care. Her book is a natural outpouring of her genuine compassion for people and her incredible work."

—Dr. Caroline Leaf, clinical neuroscientist, bestselling author, and host of
the award-winning podcast *Cleaning Up Your Mental Mess*

"In *Owning Our Struggles*, Minaa B. offers the perfect blend of empowerment and compassion, helping us reframe the thought patterns that have been keeping us stuck and giving us the tools we need to own our healing."

—Melissa Urban, *New York Times* bestselling author of
The Book of Boundaries

"Reading Minaa's book was like drinking cold water on a hot summer day. Her words are refreshing, compassionate, vulnerable, and honest. *Owning Our Struggles* provides the reader guidance while keeping them accountable. A beautiful and thought-provoking read for anyone on the journey of healing from trauma and adversity."

—Sara Kuburic, existential therapist, author of *It's On Me*,
and creator of @millennial.therapist

"Minaa is a powerful storyteller who shares insights from her background as a therapist to show how healing is possible in every phase of life. *Owning Our Struggles* provides practical tools for cultivating resilience, managing difficult relationships, and moving through loneliness. The exercises provide an engaging framework to help build mental strength and empower you wherever you are on your healing journey."

—Barb Schmidt, international bestselling author of *The Practice* and cohost of the *Barb Knows Best* podcast

"Minaa's skilled guidance in this book is soothing, powerful, and masterful. Profoundly addressing the struggles so many people face and become blocked by, this book is a must-read for anyone looking to deepen their understanding of themselves and find their way forward, toward a more whole and purposeful life. *Owning Our Struggles* is an immersive and transformative experience that will leave you prepared to reach your full potential. It's a freedom book!"

—Lalah Delia, author of *Vibrate Higher Daily*

"If you're ready to reclaim lost parts of yourself—if you're ready to come home to who you truly are—*Owning Our Struggles* is a place to begin."

—Amber Rae, author of *Choose Wonder Over Worry*

Owning Our Struggles

— A PATH TO HEALING —
AND FINDING COMMUNITY
— IN A BROKEN WORLD —

Minaa B.

A TarcherPerigee Book

an imprint of Penguin Random House LLC
penguinrandomhouse.com

Most TarcherPerigee books are available at special quantity discounts for bulk purchase for sales promotions,
premiums, fundraising, and educational needs. Special books or book excerpts also can be created
to fit specific needs. For details, write: SpecialMarkets@penguinrandomhouse.com.

ISBN (hardcover): 9780593539354
ISBN (ebook): 9780593539378

Printed in the United States of America
1st Printing

Book design by Laura K. Corless

For my family and godchildren.

Self-care is the bridge to community-care, and community-care is the bridge to community healing.

—MINAA B.

Author's Note

The stories we hold, and share, are sacred. They belong to us and deserve to be protected, and because of this, I am utterly grateful for the people who have entrusted me with their stories, which are complex, full of nuances, and filled with both grief and joy, hope and sorrow, love and pain. In order to keep these stories sacred, the names of the individuals mentioned throughout the book, as well as details of their lives, have been fictionally revised in order to protect their identities. Thank you for your understanding.

Contents

Owning
Our
Struggles

INTRODUCTION

Finding My Way

For as long as I can remember, I have felt split in half. Half Minaa, half stranger. As if I have always been both sun and moon, waiting for the moment of my eclipse. Waiting for me and my other, foreign self to collide and become one. There was always this innate feeling that something was wrong with me. I couldn't really name it, but I knew I was delicate—easy to break like fine china if yelled at too loudly, touched too harshly, looked at too angrily. The delicateness of my nature always made me feel small. I swallowed words—never spoke up. I walked with my head low—never stood tall. I tasted tears every night as I laid my face into my pillow. Always tucking and folding pain like laundry and storing it away. I spent most of my early life yearning to know *what was wrong with me.*

It wasn't until I grew older and engaged in healing work, like going to therapy, taking antidepressants, managing my mental health holistically, and studying social work, that I learned that what was wrong with me was the direct result of the things that happened to me. And although what happened to me wasn't my fault, it *was* my responsibility to heal and liberate myself from the trauma and the oppression that weighed me down. Adversity happens to everybody; there is no way to bypass difficulties in life. When, instead of running from hardship, we learn to face it head-on and lean into our difficult experiences, we gain the skills needed to become mentally strong through self-efficacy and self-advocacy. Without mental strength, we run the risk of embodying learned helplessness, which tells us that we are powerless people, but that is not true. Everyone possesses an innate power within. Healing work is all about finding the broken pieces so that you can be put back together again.

I've been a therapist for ten years now, and I earned my degree in social work from New York University. This was a big deal for my family and me, since I grew up in the hood and was raised by two immigrant parents who labored their way across borders to achieve the American dream. I was the first in my family to graduate with a college degree and went on to be the first to pursue and earn a master's degree. I remember when I was in my master's program, how I'd get on the A train from Far Rockaway toward the West 4th Street station, and the moment I got off that train, I knew to adapt. I wasn't in the hood anymore. This experience would not be like my high school. I was entering not only an elite institution but a predominantly white institution, so I knew I had to code-switch my way to the top. I struggled with the belief that I had to prove I belonged there, that I, too, was deserving of being in that space—especially since I was often one of two or three Black students in a class. I hustled even harder to be seen for more than just my skin color, to show I had the intellect to talk about more than just race, community violence, and poverty. Between doing this extra work, trying to overcome my own mental health issues, and doing the heavy lifting required to push back against oppression, I was often left feeling exhausted and even powerless. It took a lot of inner healing, mental shifting, and community-care to help me see the strength that I embodied. To see that my power was simply misplaced and that I needed to find it and claim it as a way to liberate myself.

The self-help industry has been around for decades and continues to take up significant space in the publishing sector. In 2019, the annual growth rate of self-help books reached 18.6 million. Yet historically, in the same way the mental health industry is made up primarily of white providers (86 percent, to be precise, according to the American Psychological Association), the self-help industry is dominated primarily by white authors, which leads to an erasure of not just Black, Indigenous, and People of Color (BIPOC) voices but also BIPOC readers and their experiences, healing practices, and needs. What the strength of the self-help market shows me, however, is that people want to heal, grow, and evolve. But what is self-help without advocacy, community-care, and even legislative change? We can't improve mental health without an understanding of the intersections of a person's identities as well as the structures and attitudes upheld in our society that keep people oppressed. That's why in my work, and in this book, I focus on tools that can help people work through their personal life experiences as well as the larger systems at play, from capitalism to white supremacy. The big picture is always relevant. When we subscribe to the belief that we can do the work of healing alone—which many self-help books and wellness programs suggest—we are setting ourselves up to struggle before we even begin.

I want to pause here, however, and state that this book is not only for BIPOC; this book, including the conversations about race, class, and privilege, is for everyone. You are reading a book written by a Black woman, so honoring me and my humanity is an essential part of your being able to digest the stories that I share about myself. But my expectation is not that you need to look like me in order to learn—my expectation is that you give yourself permission to honor that we are different, our experiences are different, and the way we see the world is different, and despite our differences, there is still space for listening, understanding, and holding compassion for people and their stories that do not match our own.

We are all in search of belonging, but too often we trick ourselves into believing that assimilation is belonging. To fit in, we must talk the same, act the same, look the same, and share the same identity 100 percent of the time. My job as a therapist is to recognize that my beliefs and values are mine and that I do not have permission to project them onto my clients. They are accepted and welcome to be who they are without me trying to police them and shape them into who I want them to be. I notice that this is a challenge for many people, though. Folks say they want belonging and community without realizing that they are commending assimilation and conflating oppression with justice. We will be unpacking a lot of hard truths in this book, and I need you to be willing to lean in and engage wholeheartedly when things get uncomfortable for you, because that discomfort might be a sign that some form of healing needs to take place. Give yourself permission to let it happen, because this is how we grow, and our growth is necessary not just for ourselves but for our communities.

As a clinical and community-oriented therapist, I've worked with clients who present with a variety of issues yet share similar emotional experiences, such as feeling stuck, burned out, depressed, lonely, and most upsetting, powerless.

Owning Our Struggles requires us to look within and ask: Are we truly owning who we are? No two lives are the same, but no matter our race, class status, gender, ability, or sexuality, adversity is woven deeply into the human experience. There is no amount of goodness that you can uphold that will make you exempt from struggle. Adversity will come, and how you choose to face it will play a big role in the quality of your life and mental health. However, it doesn't stop there. Self-healing may be powerful, but we are not healing to exist within a vacuum; we are healing to integrate within our community and build healthy, supportive networks. This is why community-care is so valuable and is something I will come back to again and again in this book.

I want you to take your time digesting this content like my words are crumbs and you are nibbling your way to being satiated. Healing work is heavy work, so it's not realistic to expect yourself to be ready to sort through your baggage of hurt and pain all at once. I encourage you to read this book accompanied by a journal because I will be asking you to do a lot of self-reflecting within each chapter. What I also encourage is the power of pause and giving yourself time to revisit this book over and over again in case you need to set it down when the topic becomes too heavy. It's not realistic to force yourself to do every single exercise outlined after each chapter in one sitting. It's also not realistic to force yourself to read content that might feel triggering to you. Give yourself permission to pause and take a break from time to time, and while doing so, I also want you to use discernment and apply nuanced thinking to certain areas of this book that might not be relatable to you, your experiences, or your circumstances. It is impossible for me to write a book that fits the needs of every individual reading it, so instead of trying to imagine yourself in everything I discuss or trying to project your experiences into places that do not fit, be mindful and practice being at peace with not being the intended audience for everything you consume. Allow the bits and pieces that resonate to do their work, and allow yourself to engage your imagination by holding space for the people who can actually relate, because although what you read may not be fitting for you, it might be fitting for your neighbor, partner, or friend, and community-care is learning to look beyond ourselves and not make everything about us, and instead, learning to understand the stories of others who have different experiences than we do.

I invite you to embark on a journey that will help you understand the relationship that your own healing has with the world around you. You will begin this body of work by first exploring your childhood, because I am a therapist, after all, so of course I'm going to have you reflect on your childhood and early stages of life to explore your earliest experiences, traumas, and all the things that played some kind of role in shaping who you are. As you progress through the book, you will go on a journey into adulthood and learn about the impact that certain childhood experiences may have had on your ability to create healthy connections, build emotional maturity, and develop a supportive network of peers and partners.

You will then learn about the intersection between race and mental health, and how our experiences with racism as a system that is deeply rooted in American soil has an impact on your growth and mental well-being. I urge you not to skip over this chapter if you are white because community-care requires us to learn how we sometimes inadvertently engage in cycles of harm, and we must be willing to educate ourselves and get uncomfortable to play a role in dismantling oppression and the systems that keep us disconnected and traumatized and even result in death for people of color.

Now, what is community-care if we don't talk about family, friendships, and relationships as systems that play a role in our ability to thrive or, unfortunately, sometimes play a role in the debilitation of our mental health?

You will use the information you learned in the previous chapters to help you understand how you form relationships based on your upbringing, and the current relational status that exists between you and your family. We'll unpack intergenerational trauma, emotionally immature parenting, and, most important, what to do if you want to terminate a relationship with your parents. As you work your way toward the end, you will gain tools and insight into how to find passion and purpose outside of your labor, and you will learn to harness the power of social capital and connection. Chapter 7 is full of exciting material for you to use when you find yourself feeling anxious, dysregulated, or simply need to find a way to decompress and self-soothe.

As you read through this book, you will catch my philosophy in life, which is that there is no right or wrong way to feel and no such thing as good or bad emotions. The work that I am teaching you is work that I have also done on myself, and work that I continue to do daily. I, too, had to learn that feelings are not facts, but they are not our enemy either. They exist because there is a story attached to them, and when we take the time to investigate that story with compassion and empathy, we'll see how our feelings shift and transform for the better—which has a great impact on the relationship we have with ourselves and others.

Building mental strength requires honesty, self-reflection, and vulnerability. Creating change and reclaiming community also requires honesty, self-reflection, and vulnerability. So I hope this book will grant you the courage to utilize all three. I am going to push you to step out of your comfort zone. I will ask you to examine the ways you might be playing a role in your own suffering, the oppression of self, and the oppression of others. You will need to digest some hard truths, but I guarantee it will be freeing when you get honest with yourself to make space for what you want out of life.

The good thing is that you won't have to do this work solo; I will be sharing pieces of my own personal experiences, and I will also share stories from the work that I've done with my clients. However, to protect their identities, all of their stories have been fictionally revised and altered. The point of sharing these stories is to show what community healing looks like. We are all in this together. We all face struggle and hardship, and we all have the power to overcome it. My work utilizes co-regulation and community integration as a powerful healing practice.

You have the power to do hard things.

When you're done reading this book, my hope is that you will walk away feeling empowered in a very broken world. That you will become emotionally literate and learn how to own and name your feelings and create positive change with them instead of harm (toward yourself or others). Most important, I want you to learn that there is no shame in struggling; instead of avoiding the process of healing, I hope you find the courage to embrace what feels hard and teach yourself that you have the power to do hard things, because you do!

—1—

THE STRUGGLE FOR WHOLENESS

Healing Our Inner Child, Owning Our Truth, and Reclaiming Who We Are

What we go through does not define us, but what we go through has the ability to mold and shape us. It shapes how we perceive the world, as well as our core beliefs and how we respond to adversity and conflict. We don't just wake up one morning and say, "I'm going to find ways to let people disrespect me today" or "I'm going to find all the ways to be depressed, miserable, and hate myself." Instead, it is the cumulative acts of abuse, stress, conflict, tragedy, and more that we are exposed to, whether from childhood or in adulthood, that can drive negative thinking, feelings, and behaviors, as well as how we form relationships in a social world.

A Girl Made Small

I was born into a blended family. I am my mother's second child and my father's twelfth child—making me the youngest of thirteen children. By the time I was born, most of my siblings were already adults, so as the youngest, I quickly became an observer and was always attuned to the different behaviors around me. I was in that age bracket when most adults assume, "They have no idea what's going on," so my family members never hid their conflict or anger, but what many adults fail to realize is that ages zero to five are formative years for children; they are active learners and listeners in their environment and in their critical stage of development. Kids of this age are learning their ABCs and 123s, but they are also learning about safety, love, empathy, relationships, and what it means to build healthy attachments. When exposed to unhealthy conflict rooted in physical, verbal, or emotional violence, they can absorb this as a road map for how to build and sustain relationships with themselves and others, including what they believe they should and should not tolerate.

I was always a very shy, quiet, and introverted kid. I did my best to stay out of other people's way, and because my household was always crowded, I quickly learned how to remain unnoticed and creep my way into places, then disappear like a mouse. I knew from young that too much interaction with others was overstimulating for me, and I had highly sensitive qualities, where I was always attuned to the feelings of others, which is why chaos and conflict made my stomach twist or my eyes watery on the verge of bursting into tears. I did not like drama—it literally made me feel sick, and when I began experiencing bullying, it was quite an injurious blow to my highly sensitive spirit.

Through elementary school, I was the tallest kid in my class, and that made me an easy target for many kids, who poked fun and made tall-girl jokes. Kids would ask me how many times I got left back because I always looked out of place, like I didn't belong. It's as if they were thinking, *There is no way this tall, mature-looking girl belongs in this classroom with us*, and shoot, sometimes I thought the same thing about me being surrounded by all the short kids that didn't look like me. *Like, are we really the same age? Is this where I truly belong?* Being the anomaly made making friendships hard for me. The more I was bullied, the more I was laughed at because my first inclination would be to shut down and cry, which brought on more negative attention and now crybaby jokes. I couldn't wait for school to be over so that I could run home and be free of the constant ridicule, but what I thought was my safe space no longer felt safe to me when I began to experience bullying and sibling rivalry at home.

When we think of safety for children, we often think of the parent-child relationship and the ways the parent is fostering care, nurture, and connection with their child, but what can go unnoticed or even be overlooked by parents is the impact that sibling rivalry also has on young children and how this negatively impacts their ability to form safe, healthy relationships. It's totally normal for siblings to bicker every now and then and even to have disagreements or conflict. Children do not yet have the communicative skills or emotional maturity needed to truly resolve and repair ruptures in a healthy and productive manner, and they also don't have the skills to emotionally regulate and manage their temperament the way we would expect an adult to, but when children begin to engage in emotional, physical, and sexual abuse; make threats; or begin to exert some sense of control over their sibling, this rivalry now enters abusive and manipulative territory, which is often underreported and ignored. It is most common for sibling abuse to occur with an older sibling being the perpetrator and the younger being the victim. Sibling abuse can also be directly correlated with toxic parenting, and when parents inflict abusive punishments on a child, the child may take their rage and aggression out on a sibling.

Common reasons for sibling rivalry can include:

- Parents favoring one child over the other: This can manifest as praising one child but constantly ridiculing the other or referring to one child as smart, beautiful, etc., and another as stupid, ugly, etc.

- Parents who compare their children: This can manifest as sayings that start with "Why can't you be more like your sibling?" and "You are a disgrace to the family; I wish you were more like your sibling."

At first when my sibling and I started to not get along, it was over the little things. We argued about what belonged to who and named the things the other was not allowed to touch, which often happens when you must share a room and aren't granted your own personal space, but our bickering began to evolve into my being on the receiving end of bullying. The teasing, name-calling, and grouping up with their friends to make fun of me began to make my highly sensitive self feel triggered and always activated. This ultimately began to make me annoyed, to the point of contempt and disdain, and I began to dissociate to cope with having to share a room with someone who I felt was emotionally unsafe to be around.

When children are frightened or feel unsafe, helpless, in danger, or are in overwhelming, difficult situations, they may dissociate as a survival tactic and coping mechanism. When this is happening, the child might regress into former behaviors that do not seem to fit their current developmental level, such as babbling, a more baby-like tone, or talking like someone else, either real or fictional from a cartoon or TV show. They may have an out-of-body experience where they can envision themselves disconnected from their bodies and watching themselves or what's happening around them. It is also common for children to enter a dreamlike state to detach themselves from reality. You may see some of these symptoms in teens, but teens experience additional symptoms that most children don't, like chronic forgetfulness and memory loss, especially related to the traumatic event.

To tolerate my sibling, I had to manifest a safe space in my mind and imagine that as my living space, despite our beds being less than ten feet apart. At the cost of my own emotional development, I found myself surviving by suppressing my needs, staying quiet, and tolerating mistreatment to maintain the illusion that everything was okay. That I was okay. When safety cannot be found, you create it. Survival teaches us that to preserve our well-being, we must adapt, even if we are adapting to the normalization of harm. Getting through my childhood required a sacrifice of self so that I could move through the discomfort of living with someone who was triggering to my nervous system, but that sacrifice ultimately led me down a path of debilitating mental health.

As I aged, I developed a rage that was far from the silence I had fallen into as a little kid. Suddenly my anger was a flame that could not be blown out. I remember when I was in seventh grade, my teacher told me to shut up for talking too much. Immediately, I saw red. That dysregulated little girl did not like being talked to in any old manner. It felt like an act of disrespect, and I was tired. This emotional reaction stemmed from all the years of bullying I had endured. I had had enough. I did not care if you were a child or an adult; I had reached my breaking point. In my head I thought, *Who is this woman talking to?* and I began to cuss, scream, and shout at her, practically scolding her like a child in front of all my classmates. As a result of my childhood experiences, I instantly felt threatened—even bullied—in that moment, and my body did what it knew best when it came to responding to what felt like a threat. I told her to watch her tone. I told her never to speak to me in that manner again. I also said a few other things that I am too ashamed to repeat that resulted in her crying hysterically in front of the whole classroom, then storming out. Now, imagine a twelve-year-old child making their adult teacher cry so bad they flee the classroom out of embarrassment. Once she ran out into the hallway, I already knew the kind of punishment that would await me at home.

The belt put me in my place temporarily, so I learned how to swallow my rage, even though I could taste it on my lips. *How did you become this way?* my parents would ask. *You were raised to know better, do better, be better.* They might have raised me that way, but managing my emotional impulses was not a skill I was taught. I was surrounded by sibling rivalry, long-term school bullying, dysfunctional adult relationships, and chaos. It exhausted me. It annoyed me. And eventually it wore me down. I grew up to learn that I was experiencing unaddressed depression, anxiety, and trauma, which manifested through rage, low self-esteem, and suicide ideation that eventually resulted in using cutting as a form of self-harm at age sixteen. I was broken, and I was in desperate need of healing.

Impact on the Developing Brain

The Adverse Childhood Experiences (ACEs) Study was designed to gather information on traumatic childhood experiences and their long-lasting impact on the developing adult. The issues presented in the ACEs include:

- Physical, sexual, and emotional abuse
- Physical and emotional neglect
- Intimate partner violence
- Substance abuse within the household
- Household mental illness
- Parental separation or divorce
- Incarcerated household member

A more recent version of the ACEs, called the Philadelphia ACE Survey, incorporates community-level adversity and its impact on the developing brain (in addition to the individual experiences listed above), including:

- Neighborhood safety level
- Witnessing violence: shootings, stabbings, or fights
- Hearing violence: gunshots, fights, yelling
- Being bullied at school
- Being treated poorly and disrespected by people of other cultural groups
- Experiencing racism

During my sessions with clients, I'd ask them to talk about their early life experiences. They'd describe the things that happened in the privacy of their homes but neglected to describe the things that happened outside them, like bullying in school or community violence, unless I inquired. Both experiences are powerful and will leave an emotional impact. What happens at home has the potential to drive us out into the streets, but the streets are not always a safe place. Both our home environment and community environment contribute to our origin story.

When home isn't safe, we find safety in other places. Running away from home is often the direct result of an unsafe home environment. These children are labeled as defiant when what they really may be is angry, hurt, traumatized, and afraid. Statistics from the National Runaway Safeline indicate three common reasons why young teens run away from home:

- 47 percent of children experienced conflicts with parents or guardians at home.

- 34 percent of runaways experienced sexual abuse at home (80 percent of those are girls).
- 43 percent of teens reported physical abuse as one of the main reasons they left home.

Our life experiences during our formative years can alter and influence brain development. Studies show that early experiences of trauma can leave an impact even twenty to thirty years later and affect our quality of life, education, and even romantic relationships. When a child is exposed to many of the issues presented in the ACEs, major disruptions to the different domains of development can occur, including attachment, interpersonal and peer relationships, emotional regulation, sensory integration, and overall life-functioning skills. Over time, these gaps in development can lead to major health risks, including depression, anxiety, post-traumatic stress disorder (PTSD), substance abuse, and other disruptive disorders. In addition to that, exposure to community-level violence, as listed in the Philadelphia ACEs, can result in behavioral issues such as aggression manifested through bullying, fighting, gang involvement, delinquency, and more.

Behind the scenes, so much is happening within our bodies that is directly linked to our brain. If you have been exposed to adversity and struggles since infancy and early childhood, then doing the work to become mentally strong and emotionally stabilized is not just about changing thoughts and behavior; it is about rewiring the brain. This requires a lot of inner work, which typically starts with inner-child healing.

Tuning Into the Voice of Your Inner Child

When I turned eighteen, I felt ill-equipped to be an adult. I did not enter the working world with a sense of confidence or personal responsibility. I was an adult living with a wounded child inside me, and because of that, I made terrible and unhealthy decisions that negatively impacted me and people I loved. Since I had not healed my inner child, I continued to act like my teenage self as a grown woman. But I quickly realized that if I kept treating people as if they were the source of my trauma, I would live a lonely life full of negative consequences.

You might be familiar with the phrase "Hurt people, hurt people." When we are hurting and have not done the work needed to heal, we are at risk of continuing the same cycles of dysfunctional patterns that hurt others and ourselves.

I am not five anymore. I am not sixteen. I am not eighteen. My life started to change when I realized that while what I went through as a child is extremely valid and cannot be erased, it also does not have to control me or dictate my behaviors anymore. I do not have to treat people the way I was treated. I do not have to stay stuck in the life of my five-year-old self because that is when my trauma started.

During moments of discomfort or conflict, we might find ourselves behaving like the wounded parts of ourselves because of our trauma. This can be expressed in many different forms. See if any of the behaviors below resonate with you—this could be a sign you have some inner-child healing work to do to manage your trauma responses and get unstuck from unhealthy patterns and reactions.

We tend to be quick to label the behaviors of children as defiant or as tantrums, without realizing adults throw tantrums too.

ADULT TANTRUMS CAN LOOK LIKE:

- Calling people derogatory names
- Cursing, yelling, or screaming at people
- Getting defensive and refusing to hear the other side
- Engaging in physical or verbal aggression
- Getting angry when you don't get what you want

On the other end of the spectrum, we might engage in behaviors that are not hostile, but passive. We might regress to childlike tactics that we used as coping mechanisms to keep ourselves small, safe, and secure. These behaviors can manifest as:

PEOPLE-PLEASING AND CHRONIC NICENESS:

- Being hyperfocused on what other people think about you
- Wanting to be seen as a good or nice person
- Constantly second-guessing yourself
- Putting other people's needs before your own
- Lacking insight into your identity
- Feeling responsible for other people's feelings and trying to fix or control their emotions
- Avoiding conflict
- Overapologizing and overexplaining yourself

SUBMISSIVENESS AND PASSIVITY:

- Expressing your needs poorly
- Engaging in the silent treatment: purposefully withdrawing from communication and engaging in avoidance instead of conflict resolution
- Having poor boundaries
- Lacking self-trust
- Being unable to form an opinion
- Struggling with self-validation

To thrive as healthy adults, we need to nurture our inner child. Nurturing your inner child is a way to regulate your nervous system by reminding yourself that you are safe in your body. There are things you may have needed as a child that you did not receive, but when you get back to your "window of tolerance," you will learn to give these things to yourself as an adult.

Your Window of Tolerance

When you hear the word "trauma," you might hear the term "nervous system" a lot, and that is because it plays a critical role in trauma healing and understanding trauma responses. There are two main elements related to the autonomic nervous system, which is a part of the body that regulates involuntary physiologic processes including heart rate, blood pressure, and more. These are the sympathetic nervous system—which activates the body's fight, flight, or freeze responses when it senses danger or threats—and the parasympathetic nervous system, which regulates the body and restores it to its optimal level of arousal and a state of calmness. When we experience trauma and chronic stress, the sympathetic nervous system gets activated and sometimes gets stuck in a state of hyperarousal (anxiety, panic attacks, sweating, anger, overstimulation, heavy breathing, pacing, etc.) or hypoarousal (shutting down, freezing, dissociation, numbing, poor emotional processing, depression, fatigue, etc.). When stress and trauma are ongoing, the nervous system can become conditioned to remain in either one of these states, leaving a person to consistently exhibit the symptoms associated with hyper- or hypoarousal even when not faced with danger or a threat.

Your window of tolerance is the window where your nervous system is in a state of healthy arousal, and getting back to it is another way to tend to your inner child. Luckily, there are practices that you can do on your own to help activate the parasympathetic nervous system.

I find that many of us struggle with naming our emotions. When I held sessions with clients and asked them how they were doing, they would respond, "I'm good." And I'm quite sure you are guilty of this as well. Here's the thing: "good" is not an emotion. Lots of people use "good" as a descriptor of their feelings when deep down inside, they are angry, hurt, sad, or even suicidal. Naming our feelings is an important practice and plays a critical role in building emotional intelligence, but sometimes naming an emotion in the moment can be difficult, especially when your body is in a state of hypo- or hyperarousal. Instead of labeling your feelings with an emotion, a quick way to do a self-check-in is to ask yourself how you are feeling on a scale of 1 to 10. One is feeling your lowest and 10 is feeling your greatest. If you find that you are feeling a 5 or below, it can be beneficial to engage in self-soothing techniques and practices for brain and body healing.

PRACTICES TO CALM YOUR NERVOUS SYSTEM:

- **Move your body:** This includes cardio, walking, yoga, stretching, dance, karate, a sport, or any kind of movement that you can engage in to release endorphins and increase serotonin, hormones that induce feelings of happiness and help decrease stress.

- **Rewatch an old TV show or movie:** When the body is activated in a fight, flight, or freeze mode, it is looking for something nonthreatening to help stabilize itself. As a result, you might find yourself feeling constantly overstimulated, and since trauma hijacks the brain, trying to think your way through stress might be difficult. A great way to calm your nervous system is to expose yourself to something that is both safe and familiar. I tend to watch reruns of *The Office* frequently, and no matter how many times I watch Michael Scott hit Meredith with his car, I can't help but to laugh with intensity. During these moments my brain is releasing dopamine, which is the "feel-good" hormone, helping to calm my nervous system. You can also look through old pictures and photo albums that evoke positive memories or listen to old music associated with a celebration or positive event.

- **Box breathing:** Wonder why you always hear about breathing exercises as a mental health tool? Well, that is because no matter where you go, you take your body with you. You will not always have access to tangible tools and remedies, but you will *always* have your body, and our breath is one of the greatest gifts the body has to offer. You can engage in a variety of breathing practices to self-soothe and bring yourself back to your equilibrium. The box breathing method can be done anywhere at any time. First, focus on your breath. Then inhale for four seconds, hold your breath for four seconds, exhale for four seconds, and hold that space for four seconds before you inhale again. While you do the breathing exercise, you will imagine creating the shape of a box as you inhale, hold, exhale, hold.

- **Co-regulation:** Trying to get through a trauma-inducing event alone can be difficult. Sometimes we have it in us to regulate ourselves, and other times we need someone else's nervous system to help us with repairing our own. You can engage in co-regulation by doing the previous practices with someone, as well as engaging in a hug or a healthy conversation, working out with a partner, or simply spending quality time with someone who is emotionally and physically safe for you.

Boundaries to Meet the Needs
of Your Inner Child

Boundaries are about setting limits with ourselves, and others, to effectively manage our time, feel safe in our relationships, preserve our energy, and have our needs met. Most important, boundaries help us with regulating our nervous system. A lack of boundaries can lead to issues like stress, anxiety, mental health issues, and dysfunctional relationships. Ultimately, boundaries are an act of self-care and self-advocacy.

As a child, you had to rely on your caregiver to determine what your needs were and then provide for you, but if you were raised by emotionally immature, absent, or abusive parents, you may be accustomed to not having your needs met and feel unsure about or even afraid of speaking up, setting expectations, and advocating for the things that you want. As an adult, you are your own best advocate. You get to decide what makes you feel safe—or not. Knowing your boundaries is where your agency and autonomy lie. Asserting your needs is the first step in healing the inner child who did not have their needs met.

Where Do We Need Boundaries?

Through the ABC model, which is rooted in cognitive behavioral therapy—a modality that is used to help people understand the relationship between their thoughts and feelings and how it impacts behavior—you can examine your triggers and responses to develop greater awareness of where you may need to set a boundary, either with yourself or with others. Let's take a look.

A—Activating event
- What or who triggered you?

B—Beliefs, both explicit and implicit
- What are the positive and negative thoughts you have about the activating event or person?

C—Consequences (positive or negative) that manifest both behaviorally and emotionally
- How did you react behaviorally?
- How did you react emotionally?
- How did your body respond (e.g., shutting down, dissociation, fatigue)?

Boundary: What needs to be done differently? What boundary can you erect as a way to safeguard yourself from the negative effects of the activating event?

Back when I was in college, I formed a friendship with someone who, in many ways, had behaviors that mimicked one of my family members. It left me emotionally exhausted but also irritated, to say the least. They, of course, were not aware of the impact their behaviors had on me, and I often felt bad addressing them, because I didn't want to hurt their feelings.

As time went on, however, I felt drained, and I knew I needed to find the courage to speak up and set a boundary to safeguard myself from their actions but to also give them an opportunity to see how their behaviors had impacted me. I applied the ABC model to establish boundaries.

A—Activating Event: This friend had a habit of asking for favors, a lot of them, and the asking often wasn't the issue; it was the fact that they never showed up for me, ever, and this imbalance made our relationship one-sided. I was always giving; they were always taking. The more they took, the angrier I became.

B—Beliefs: I wanted to be nice. I thought giving more than I could was an act of loyalty and kindness, when in fact it was people-pleasing and a search for external validation that I mattered to someone. I needed people to see the value in keeping me around, which stemmed from my lack of self-worth and ultimately kept enabling the problematic behaviors that drained me.

C—Consequence: As a result of giving continuously because I wanted to be seen as "nice," I was always left tired, upset, drained, and empty—this was the negative consequence of my inability to say no. Even if I felt like this friend should have known better, it was still my responsibility to pay attention to their patterns and speak up to inform them how I felt about their behaviors. This made me realize it was time to develop and state my boundaries.

A boundary with myself looked like: "I will honor my needs by saying no to the things that I don't want to do for my friend."

A boundary with my friend looked like: "No, I cannot do this favor for you" or "I am unable to help you out this time."

Boundaries teach us that we are not powerless people. We do not have to glide through life with a false sense of hopelessness. We are people who have the power to make healthy choices and changes to suit our needs.

Knowing Where Your Boundaries Lie

Now that we understand how to use the ABC model to assess where a boundary is needed, you may be wondering how exactly to implement the boundary and where. There are five areas in your life that Boundaries fall into:

- **Physical:** Our physical boundaries refer to our bodies but also to our physical space. When the coronavirus pandemic hit, in many stores, indicators were placed on the floor signaling people to stand six feet apart. Not only did this practice encourage social distancing, but it also helped encourage boundaries because we tend to violate people's physical space even without touching them. Examples of physical boundaries can be:
    - "I prefer not to hug, but I don't mind giving a handshake."
    - "Please take your shoes off as you enter into my home."

- **Emotional:** It's hard being vulnerable around judgmental people. An emotional boundary is setting a parameter around what you need to feel emotionally safe. This is an area worth exploring. What are the things that make you feel safe, and most important, which people make you feel safe? Examples of emotional boundaries can look like:
    - "I'm not ready to share more information regarding what happened to me, but I appreciate your concern."
    - "Please don't share this information with anyone else in the family. I'd like for this to stay between us."

- **Time:** A poor use of time leads to poor health and lots of stress. Time boundaries simply allow you to make better use of your time by managing the things you prioritize and give your energy to. You cannot go to a bank to withdraw time; you have only the hours that you have, so stop treating time like something you can duplicate. Examples of time boundaries are:
    - "I will wake up at 6:00 a.m. to have time for journaling before my kids wake up."
    - "I will cut off the TV at 9:00 p.m. to go to bed on time so that I can stop waking up feeling tired."

- **Sexual:** This type of boundary helps build physical and emotional intimacy. Sexual boundaries establish rules around what makes you feel safe sexually. This means consent to engage in sex, but it doesn't stop there. Even when you have consent to engage in sex, you also need consent to engage in certain kinks and sexual practices. Examples of sexual boundaries look like:

- "I prefer to get STD/HIV tests if we are going to begin having unprotected sex."
- "There's this practice that I would like to try, but I want to know if you are comfortable with it first."

- **Intellectual:** We all have different thoughts, ideas, and perspectives. When in conversation, we may find ourselves expressing differences, and boundaries are a great way to acknowledge that differences can be honored without resorting to disrespect. Examples of intellectual boundaries look like:
  - "I notice we have very different views when it comes to this topic, and your views have me feeling a bit uneasy. I'm going to disengage from this conversation and consider how we move forward from here."
  - "When I share my thoughts with you, it hurts when you laugh or poke fun at me just because you don't like my ideas."

Now that you know the five areas in your life where you can erect boundaries, you can begin assessing who you need a boundary with and where. Do you need to set an emotional boundary with your partner because they tend to raise their voice during arguments? Do you need to set a physical boundary with your mother-in-law because she has a tendency to show up at your house uninvited? Maybe you need to set a time boundary with your manager, who tends to pile work tasks on you to complete during the last five minutes of your shift.

Setting limits with others can be intimidating, especially when the boundary is family, because family patterns run deep. I created a technique called the BEST method to help you emotionally prepare for boundary setting, so that you can do your best to remain assertive in the moment.

B—Boundary
- What is the boundary that you plan to set? And with who?

E—Emotional awareness
- What emotional responses are you experiencing as a result of wanting to set this boundary (e.g., guilt, anxiety, fear)?

S—Self-soothing
- What self-soothing technique(s) will you use to regulate these emotions (e.g., meditation, deep breathing, grounding exercises, journaling)?

T—Alternative thoughts
- What negative thoughts are you experiencing?
- Are they rational or irrational?
- What is an alternative positive thought for every negative one?

Emotional awareness: When I determined the boundary I needed to set with my friend, I started to feel flooded with fear, worry, and even guilt. I was concerned that I would hurt their feelings and lose our friendship. Because I was aware of the strong emotions the boundary was bringing up for me, I sought ways to self-regulate to prep myself to feel confident in saying no.

Self-soothing: Writing and audio journaling were my safety net. They were how I released my fearful and guilty thoughts. Getting words out on paper or saying them out loud helped me catch distortions in my thinking and be more compassionate toward myself.

Alternative thoughts: For every negative scenario I thought of, I came up with a positive one to replace it. For instance, my big fear was that my friend would be upset with me. I reminded myself that I have the ability to handle discomfort, and someone else's anger is not my responsibility to fix. I can have compassion for my friend and their feelings without trying to fix or erase their feelings.

Setting boundaries can feel hard, especially when you have to set them with difficult people. This work takes time, so don't put too much pressure on yourself to become a pro overnight. You will always find yourself in new scenarios and experiences where you are discovering and adjusting your boundaries. Most important, your window of tolerance will always alert you when it's time to set a boundary for the sake of your nervous system and emotional health, which is why planning and assessing your boundaries in advance can give you the tools you need to push back against emotional control and not stay stuck in your fears.

Your fearful inner child might try to resort to self-protecting through people-pleasing tendencies, submission, or even engaging in silence. But remember that your inner child is safe within you! You have the agency to ask for what you need. By self-soothing, you can regulate yourself when you feel emotionally flooded, so you can make decisions that are rooted in logic and not just pure emotion. Our inner child deserves to feel loved, nurtured, and safe. Setting boundaries teaches us healthy methods of self-protection and will help you in the work of defining your core beliefs and values.

Defining Your Beliefs and Values

Our core beliefs are like the soil of the earth, and our thoughts are the seeds that we plant. What grows depends on whether the soil is healthy or rotted. Our beliefs determine how we interpret our experiences and interactions with others.

Because we are born into a world where rules already exist and within families that have their own unique way of being, our core beliefs and values are generally shaped by our family traditions and cultural structures. As we enter adulthood, we might notice that some of the things we were taught as children, such as how to raise a kid or what it means to be successful, start to shift and change. When we grow up dealing with adversity and negative experiences, we can develop negative core beliefs.

NEGATIVE CORE BELIEFS LOOK LIKE:

- "I am not good enough."
- "I'm unlovable."
- "No one can be trusted."
- "X group of people is dangerous."
- "No one has the ability to change."
- "I am not worthy of good things."
- "Life is stupid and meaningless."
- "I am worthless."

Experiencing bullying from a very young age deeply impacted my self-esteem. I grew up believing that I wasn't beautiful and that I was unlovable. When it came time for me to form relationships, I engaged in some of the people-pleasing habits I listed earlier in the chapter. I was always overextending myself with others because I wanted to be seen as a valuable and contributing member of my social groups. When I wasn't overcommitting, I was overachieving. My lack of self-worth pushed me to excel in school and get good grades because I knew I would be praised for something. The deep sense of worthlessness I carried caused me to believe that I could earn love from my parents and earn respect in my social settings by being the kid who graduated early from both high school and undergrad and could boast the name NYU wherever I went. But chasing accolades never fulfills an empty soul. It took a lot of unlearning for me to recognize how my negative core beliefs were driving me to detrimental behaviors that caused me to play a role in my own suffering.

The same way you have the agency to set boundaries and express your needs, you also get to decide your values and core beliefs. These no longer need to come from your caregivers or the environment in which you were raised. They are up to you and will determine how you continue to evolve as an adult.

In order to live in your truth, you need to know what you believe in, what is important to you, who you are, and how you want to contribute to the world. You have the power to change what isn't working for you.

To do the work of defining your beliefs and values, consider these questions:

- What is most important to me? (Think of all areas of your life: family, career, friendships, money, time, location, hobbies, and passions.)
- How do I honor and make time for the things that are important to me?
- How do I define respect? And how am I upholding this in how I allow people to treat me, as well as how I treat others?
- Are my beliefs mine, or am I operating by someone else's blueprint? Whose? And why?
- Are my everyday actions currently in alignment with what I claim to believe? What do I need to start doing differently to live in alignment with my goals?
- Do my beliefs keep me stuck, or do they propel me forward? Do they honor the humanity of others, or do they play into the dehumanization of others?

- Do my beliefs serve to elevate my well-being, or do they negatively impact my mental health?

When we start asking ourselves the real questions, the ones that make us curious and put us face-to-face with the flawed parts of ourselves, we are then able to do the work of honoring who we truly are. But to grow and heal, you must be the one to figure out which areas of your life need to change.

Forgiveness and Compassion

In my past, I made choices that don't align with my current core beliefs and values. These choices resulted in both self-harm and harm to others. I have since learned that although I may not be able to go back in time and change my actions, I can do the work of learning and unlearning as well as being committed to changing my behavior in the present. I can do better now that I know better. The only way I have been able to do this is through self-compassion and forgiveness.

Practicing self-forgiveness is vital for healing. Self-forgiveness does not mean forgetting. It is not an undoing of your past actions, nor does it mean getting a pass on your harmful behaviors. You will still face consequences for your actions. Self-forgiveness means opening our eyes to our actions and seeing them clearly without the cloud of shame

> Practicing self-forgiveness is vital for healing.

or denial. We can't move forward when we are gripped by the weight of shame, and when we aren't moving forward, we are at risk for recycling old patterns and behaviors that can lead to further harm. In the words of Brené Brown, "Shame corrodes the very part of us that believes we are capable of change."

PRACTICING SELF-FORGIVENESS LOOKS LIKE:

- Acknowledging the mistakes you've made
- Owning the consequences that resulted from your choices
- Committing to changed behavior, not just for the other person, but also for others and yourself
- Owning your guilt and not treating it as a character flaw
- Apologizing to yourself for not knowing better
- Apologizing to yourself for knowing better and choosing not to do better

Self-compassion is the foundation of self-forgiveness. We are flawed, imperfect human beings, which means we will make mistakes in life, and unfortunately some of those mistakes might cost us deeply. Dr. Kristin Neff writes in her book *Self-Compassion: The Proven Power of Being Kind to Yourself*, "To give ourselves compassion, we first have to recognize that we are suffering." It can be hard to be compassionate toward your own suffering, but this work is necessary because everything we do reflects our own inner world. We can meet others only where we have met ourselves. If we are not willing to go the distance, we run the risk of standing still in shame, hurt, and suffering.

PRACTICING SELF-COMPASSION LOOKS LIKE:

- Being kind to yourself when you get things wrong
- Allowing yourself not to be perfect
- Showing yourself kindness and patience
- Being accepting of your flaws and shortcomings
- Being understanding when you mess up
- Nurturing yourself through positive self-talk
- Being nonjudgmental and less self-critical

Self-compassion is also vital for inner-child healing. You may have grown up so used to being punished for existing that you believe you are unworthy of care, kindness, and gentleness. But you can now give yourself the compassion you didn't receive as a child. This unlocks something deep within that has been yearning for love and connection. You have the ability to give yourself what you've been missing. You have the ability to meet your own needs. Think about the power you hold.

> **You have the ability to give yourself what you've been missing.**

It's worth stating that healed people are not immune from hurting others. We are all human first, and even good people can cause harm. The difference is that healed people have learned the skill of taking ownership for their wrongs and holding themselves accountable, while staying compassionate to themselves and others. That is what healing work is: awakening to personal responsibility and making the choice to do better, grow, and evolve.

As we unpack trauma healing in the next chapter, the power of inner-child healing, boundaries, compassion, and forgiveness will remain critical components to your healing and ability to form community. The exercises that follow are meant to anchor you in this work before we move on.

Exercises

Complete the following exercise by practicing audio journaling. Grab your phone, press the Record button, and answer the following prompts out loud. Listen intently to your response when you're done, and replay this as an affirmation to remind yourself of your process.

- Finish the sentence: "I hold the power to . . ."
- Finish the sentence: "I am forgiving myself for . . ."

When we are plagued by negative thoughts and triggers from our past, it is important and healthy to have an outlet where we can freely express our needs and talk about our struggles. One of the simplest ways to do this is by note-taking or talking out loud. This practice allows us to get our feelings out and examine our experiences through an objective lens, rather than through the lens of distorted or preexisting beliefs. Which is why audio journaling is an exercise I frequently recommend to clients (and do often myself).

To take this exercise to the next level outside of the prompts I provided, take five to ten minutes to record yourself talking freely about an event or interaction that upset you. Get it all out. Then listen to the recording to assess whether there are any discrepancies, the same way you would listen to a friend and give them advice to help them discern between rational and irrational thoughts. And if hearing your own voice feels too daunting, you can always eventually switch this practice to journaling and writing your thoughts down instead.

Can you hear how your inner child impacts your thoughts or reactions? Do you have more clarity on the situation and yourself? What did you learn about your way of thinking after playing the audio back?

— 2 —

THE STRUGGLE FOR HEALING

Developing Emotional Maturity and Resilience, and Growing in the Face of Adversity

Healing Is a Social Justice Issue

As a therapist, I am a huge advocate for therapy, which shouldn't come as a surprise. I believe therapy is the emotional first aid a lot of folks need when it comes to navigating a deeply flawed world as well as the inner workings of our humanity. As people, we are always exposed to adversity. There is no way to bypass hardship in life, and having an outlet where we can talk about the emotional injuries we endure can bring ease, peace, and healing into our lives. However, I want to be real, and as a therapist, what I also want people to know is that therapy has its limits; it is not structured to help you heal from *all* your problems. We need numerous resources for healing, not just therapy.

The world of therapy is tied to mental health, so in many ways we expect therapy to be the thing that can help us heal from the multiple issues that *impact* our mental health, but this is not always the case. And that is because emotional injuries that impact our mental health do not just come from challenging childhoods, acute trauma, and interpersonal conflicts; they are also deeply tied to structural issues and social inequities. Therapy will not help you pay your rent if you are financially insecure. Therapy will not take you out of poverty and give you a livable working wage. Therapy will not put an end to police brutality. Therapy is not going to help you meet your basic needs and provide you with food, shelter, and safety. Therapy falls under health care and isn't even easily accessible through the American health-care system. I advocate for healing, but we cannot pretend that healing isn't a social justice issue, because it absolutely is. Healing goes beyond our tendency toward individualism and requires structural change in many ways.

A few years ago I worked as a mental health consultant at a school in Queens, New York. I was introduced to a parent I'll call Denise for the sake of protecting her identity. Denise was twenty years old and had two small children enrolled in the school. Although she and I were being formally introduced for the first time, I already knew of her from the numerous complaints teachers had regarding her attitude and her constant outbursts, in which she would curse out the staff or even get into conflict with other parents. When the program director introduced me to her, I thought she'd be resistant to meeting me, but instead, she seemed hungry for connection and expressed being happy to have someone to talk to.

In our intimate time together, I learned a lot about Denise. She was unemployed and had tried to secure work, but finding something that would allow her to drop her kids off on time and pick them up always presented a struggle. Her kids' father was absent, and she didn't have anyone she considered a support system. Denise needed someone to talk to. Someone to help her cope with her stressors of finding a job; securing stable housing, as she was living uncomfortably with her aunt in a tiny apartment that didn't have enough room for her and her children; and earning money for clothes, food, and other resources to meet her and her kids' basic needs. What Denise needed was help that therapy could not give her: she needed resources and community-care.

When I tried to connect Denise to resources, she found herself jumping through hoops and navigating cycles that were both exhausting and taxing on her mental health. A single mother, Denise was navigating the world as a young, poor Black woman who was both socially and economically disadvantaged, and she was doing it all alone. She didn't have friends, and both of her parents were deceased, so she had been raised by her aunt as well as her older siblings, who since had moved on with their own lives to take care of their own families. Now it was just Denise and her aunt, who was much older than Denise and unable to support her in the ways she needed. What Denise did have, however, was the staff at the school who knew of her circumstances and cared about her well-being. That was her village, and that place had become her home.

The Many Faces of Adversity and Trauma

When I was growing up, I always thought trauma equaled war and veterans. Then I went to graduate school and learned about the inner workings of trauma in a more robust way, though it was still somewhat limited. What I was taught in class and trainings centered around distressing interpersonal events like child abuse, domestic violence, sexual assault or abuse, emotional and physical neglect, and more. I also learned about war and natural disasters. What I did not learn about, however, was how social inequities can be a form of complex trauma for individuals who must navigate the many systems of oppression, especially when they are a part of a marginalized group.

In chapter 1, I talked about the ACEs and the revised Philadelphia ACEs study that gives us insight into the traumatic experiences a person may have dealt with during their upbringing, but trauma is not just a childhood issue and can manifest in many ways even during adulthood.

THIS CAN BE TRAUMATIC:

- Having a miscarriage
- Infertility
- Death of a loved one
- Losing a job
- A global pandemic
- Mass shootings

AND THIS CAN ALSO BE TRAUMATIC:

- Food apartheid
- Racial profiling
- Police brutality

- Gentrification and housing displacement
- Experiencing redlining
- Medical racism
- Gender oppression

And that list can run on forever when we include all the isms: ageism, sexism, classism, and ableism as well as homophobia, transphobia, xenophobia, and so on.

Dealing with these issues can be a form of complex trauma because they are usually not isolated incidents. Trauma cycles can be broken down into three types:

- **Acute:** A single distressing event that does not reoccur (e.g., the 9/11 terrorist attack)
- **Chronic:** Repeated and prolonged exposure to a distressing event (e.g., child neglect or abuse, bullying, community violence, etc.)
- **Complex:** Exposure to multiple traumatic events that are prolonged, severe, and pervasive (e.g., different forms of child abuse, racism, domestic violence, etc.)

Healing is a social justice issue because trauma impacts not only the individual but the family unit, our communities, and the social and economic structure of our country. A research study conducted by Michal Gilad, a Penn Law doctoral student and an associate fellow with the University of Pennsylvania Leonard Davis Institute of Health Economics, and Abraham Gutman, an economist and health policy expert, shared that adverse childhood outcomes that result from a lack of treatment cost society more than $458 billion each year, with a lifetime tally of $194,000 per individual. In Gilad's own research, survey results showed that in most states, resources were available for children who experienced abuse, and they were eligible for compensation for therapeutic services; however, being a parent from a disadvantaged community made it difficult to navigate these resources because of language and economic barriers. With formal education and a doctoral degree, Gilad had the resources, finances, and education to understand the law, as well as to navigate other barriers that could arise, whereas the average person, especially a disadvantaged person, does not.

Gilad's research also dives into the social and economic costs of unhealed and untreated childhood trauma. When examining the snowball effect of childhood trauma and exposure to violence and crime, we must consider how trauma impacts a child's overall health, including their intellectual health, which leads to issues like school absences, suspensions, and even expulsion, as well as the possibility of dropping out altogether as the child ages. Once academic scores suffer and a child's intellectual health is stunted, their ability to secure a job or stable career is impacted, which affects not only the child but their families, community, and most important, society, by placing a financial burden on systems such as education, child welfare, social services, law enforcement, and so on. The only way to cut back on these costs is to create better systems, which could even require the total demolition of our policies and practices to redesign legislation that considers individuals who are disadvantaged in the first place.

I remember having a conversation with my supervisor, who was a

Black woman, about how frustrated I was with the constant difficulties I was presented with when trying to match Denise, as well as many of my other disadvantaged clients, with resources to get them the help they needed. I said to her, "Our system is broken and it's frustrating." And I will never forget when she turned to me and said, "Our system isn't broken. It was designed this way and it's functioning exactly how it was intended to."

Mental health care is not just therapy; it is also public policy. Recovery cannot happen just while you are sitting on your therapist's couch. It's a starting point, but it will not always be enough. No matter how good I was at my job, there was no way that I alone was going to help Denise rise out of poverty and overcome the social inequities she was burdened by. Having access to resources, not just tangible but geographical and financial, was a priority for Denise and often took months to secure. Denise, however, is not the only person who is disproportionately disadvantaged in society; there are so many more who are probably unsure of where to start or who do not have access to the people and community who can give them the insight to know where to look for help even if they are interested in seeking it. Mental health recovery requires community, accessibility and affordability, and comprehensive care. Organizations like NAMI, Mental Health America, and Be Vocal: Speak Up make it easy for individuals to learn how they can play a role in policy changes that can do just that: create social and economic change. You can play your part by doing things like voting and educating yourself on the policymakers you are voting for; reaching out through phone or email to your electoral officials with concerns as well as ideas for change; reading up on policy in general, especially at your school and job; and joining pledges created by these organizations above that are helping to fight for change in the mental health sphere. Lasting change is not just about what we do for ourselves; it's also about what we do for the communities that we are a part of.

When the Grass Looks Greener
but It's Actually Not

I once worked with a client who told me that her mother would constantly remind her that she was the same age as Ariana Grande to imply that she should be further ahead in life and more successful than she was. I knew a lot of folks like her mother. The ones who measure success by external outcomes, with little regard for social and economic influences such as race, class, gender, and able-bodied privileges. There are folks like her mother, who believe comparison is a good pep talk. If I remind you of how much you lack, it will make you work harder to alleviate the shame being induced, and we live in a culture where many folks still believe that hard labor is all it takes to be successful, without considering the privileges mentioned above and more. What also needs to be accounted for, something that is often overlooked, is how success for many starts in childhood. As I've stated in chapter 1 and earlier in this chapter, people who experience chronic or complex trauma at a young age may already be at a disadvantage because childhood trauma can have a twenty- to thirty-year impact on the developing brain, injuring mental, emotional, intellectual, and physical health. So trying to measure yourself up to someone who is already socially and economically ahead of you, and who also experienced minimal adverse childhood experiences while having multiple privileges, is honestly an unfair comparison. What's also worth exploring is that success is subjective. There is no fair way to measure success because success can be defined only by each of us individually. Success as a social construct is often tied to fame, wealth, and a person's relationship status, hence why my former client's mother thought Ariana Grande was an embodiment of success and not her own daughter, who just so happened to accomplish way more than her own mother did in life. Within this framework, there is no way societal standards are going to keep us elevated and place us in a position to thrive when they're rooted in not just toxicity but white supremacy and patriarchal views.

While working with my client Denise, it was clear that she, too, struggled with measuring up to others and had low self-esteem. She would always compare herself to other people in her age bracket as well as to the other mothers she would see dropping off their children every day. The more she watched, the more she loathed herself, and she was often filled with a righteous anger but also a heavy sadness for her own circumstances. She'd talk to me about the death of her parents and how she wished she had a different life. She'd envision what her life would be like if she didn't have so many setbacks. And the more she dreamed, the more she began to feel bad about venting her frustration.

"Maybe I'm stuck because I complain too much," she'd said to me once. "My life isn't that bad compared to other people." And she went on to talk about how there are people all over the world who have it much harder than her, even other mothers who frequented the school. I responded, "Although it's true that there are people who have it much harder, that doesn't negate that you also have it hard too."

Denise had learned that to distance herself from her reality, she could slip into someone else's world, and by doing so, sometimes she ended up in a world that felt much harder than her own. The grass isn't always greener, but sometimes we look over other people's fences because we are not satisfied with where we are standing.

The truth is, it's okay to want more. Wanting more for yourself does not mean you are ungrateful for the life you have. We grow because we know greater versions of ourselves exist, and we don't have to limit our potential. Expansion is a beautiful thing, and it doesn't have to be constrained.

Comparative suffering, however, limits our growth. When we fixate on what's happening to others—to the point where we pull out our measuring sticks to assess whether we have the right to be unhappy, frustrated, sad, or suffering—we deny the existence of our own hurt and minimize our pain just because others have it harder. It leads to an immense feeling of guilt, assuming we did something bad for wanting more just because others have less than what we currently have or are facing adversity in areas of their lives where we are currently comfortable or at peace. Let me ask you something, though. When was the last time your guilt actually changed someone's life? Did your guilt elevate someone else? Or did it just keep you stuck in a state of chronic self-pity?

Denise had a right to be frustrated with her life. While it may have been true that there were other people who were in need and dealing with their own traumas, it didn't mean that her pain could not be loud or that she had to shrink herself because she wasn't worse off.

Our difficult experiences do not disappear when we detach ourselves from our emotions. Denying our truth, because we have been exposed to someone else's truth, doesn't make our truth less factual. What this does is cut us off from empathy, care, and understanding, because we are too busy ranking other people's lives and determining how much compassion they deserve based on how difficult their circumstances are.

COMMON SIGNS OF COMPARATIVE SUFFERING INCLUDE:

- **Bitterness:** A feeling of unfairness, which causes you to treat others with contempt or even disrespect due to your own anger related to your circumstances
- **Withdrawal:** Distancing yourself from others who have it either better or worse because they evoke uncomfortable feelings related to your own suffering
- **Quitting:** Giving up on yourself because you don't see a point in trying to do better or you believe your circumstances won't change, especially when other people you know are still stuck in their suffering
- **Lack of gratitude:** Finding it difficult to be grateful for things in life because you are fixated on what others have that you lack
- **Anxiety:** Constant worry or rumination related to what's going wrong for you and others, with little attention to what's going right
- **Guilt:** Feeling bad for being able to overcome hardship or evolve in certain areas of life, such as relationships, finances, and so on, because other people are suffering

When Positivity Becomes Toxic

As we journey, it's both normal and common to try to make sense of our pain and suffering. When Denise spoke to me about her childhood, it was as if she had spent her life trying to piece together a puzzle that she realized had too many missing pieces; she knew that she would most likely spend the rest of her life not knowing the why behind many of the childhood experiences she had. Such as why her parents died when she was young. Although her siblings played a role in raising her, Denise didn't have a close relationship with many of them, which left her feeling disconnected from others. All she had was herself, not even a close friend she could call and vent to, other moms she could have playdates with, or a community of people to share jokes with, bond with, or lean on for comfort and to feel nestled in the warmth of connection. Denise wandered the hallways of the school because that place was home for her. That building was a place of safety and comfort; it was where she found meaning for herself. It was the place that kept her grounded.

I'd watch the many ways Denise would try to cultivate friendships with others. The way she looked at the other mothers when she said hello or how she'd listen with ears hungry for information whenever a parent workshop was happening. Denise wanted more, but there were many hoops she'd have to jump through to get where she was trying to go. On occasion, when Denise and I would speak, I could sense through her body language when something was wrong. She'd bounce her leg more, her eyes would wander away from mine to the floor repeatedly, and she'd kiss her teeth every now and then as she talked, all while telling me she was "fine" and how "great" she was feeling. I'd ask her who she was trying to convince she was okay, me or her? And in response she'd roll her eyes at me, annoyed at me for calling her bluff and not letting her get away with lying to herself or even me. Denise wanted to be able to say she was fine and that she was doing great, but she wasn't, and she often needed to be reminded that there is no shame in acknowledging that as the truth. Denise was tired, and she had a right to be, but trying to force herself to be happy when she knew she wasn't was not going to lead her on a path to happiness; instead it made her more miserable because she kept having to suppress the truth of her sadness, anger, and frustration to present herself as happy, joyful, and grateful.

Trying to always remain happy is not only destructive but unrealistic. Emotions are not pieces of clothing that we can sort through and put on and take off when we feel like it. They are a by-product of our experiences, a reaction to stimuli, and how we interpret those experiences and the impact they have on the brain. Though there is data to support a variety of core emotions, the basic six emotions we all experience are anger, fear, surprise, disgust, joy, and sadness. Consider these the parent emotions, and other feelings, like jealousy, depression, annoyance, frustration, and so on, are the children of one of these basic emotions.

The first myth about emotions that needs to be dispelled is that emotions are either good or bad. This myth has caused people to believe that it is distasteful to experience emotions such as jealousy or harmful to experience emotions such as anger or rage. The truth is, emotions are not harmful, but what we choose to do with our emotions can be. When emotions are not processed, or when we do not have healthy coping mechanisms in place to manage our emotions, it can lead to problematic behaviors that hurt others as well as ourselves. The inability to cope with our emotions can often come from judging our emotions. When we label emotions as bad, we assume we are bad people for feeling them instead of learning to accept and embrace that our feelings exist on a spectrum and the presence of an emotion has nothing to do with our value, worth, or morality. By labeling feelings, we put some on a pedestal and treat them as deities. We worship and crave happiness because we no longer see the value in rage and sadness. We've been taught these emotions are crippling to the spirit, useless, and even futile. This detachment from negative feelings causes us to overlook the value of the messages our feelings are trying to send us.

Every feeling has power and purpose. Blocking off certain emotions because we think they are bad means we are not stopping to investigate the intricacies of our humanity. Anger, rage, and sadness are not detached from passion and joy as much as we think they are. These emotions exist as storytellers. They signal to us that harm has been caused, and in some way, we feel as if we've been injured either physically, spiritually, or emotionally. Sadness and anger open our eyes to our own personal injustices, including the injustices of the world. If we choose to cut these emotions off, we are also choosing to turn a blind eye to the inequities happening to us and around us. I often think about these small but powerful words by singer Solange: "I got a lot to be mad about."

Every feeling has power and purpose.

Life is not always bliss; it is as full of darkness as it is of light. Giving ourselves permission to fold when necessary, instead of always trying to be strong and smile while our hurt is tearing us up on the inside, is how we free ourselves from this self-oppression that is constantly weighing us down. Nobody gets a badge of honor for how happy they can be all the time. All this self-oppressed suffering for nothing. No reward. No prosperity. Just more misery, pain, and agony that eventually tear down both the mind and the body. We spend our days striving for happiness, not realizing that the road to happiness requires us to have a deeper sense of knowledge and understanding for why our rage and despondency exist in the first place. If you aren't willing to explore the crevices and cracks of your suffering, you will struggle to reach wholeness.

Toxic positivity culture is also at fault for why many people have a hard time honoring and owning their emotions. It is a culture rooted in the desire to be positive all the time, no matter how tragic an experience is. Toxic positivity is shedding a light on how difficult it has become for many of us to honor and own our struggles, and the difficult emotions attached to those struggles. When we get to a place where we are encouraging people to be happy and find the silver lining in issues like poverty or racism, or even personal wounds such as having a miscarriage, losing a loved one or a job, or being diagnosed with an illness, it shows that we are becoming more and more disconnected from ourselves and others. We are deeply in need of nurturing ourselves in order to know how to nurture others, instead of being another source of stress or disheartenment in a time of what might feel like emotion turmoil.

TOXIC POSITIVITY SOUNDS LIKE:

- Telling someone "Everything happens for a reason" or "Look on the bright side" when they are dealing with tragedy

- Minimizing people's problems by saying, "It could be worse"
- Telling someone to be strong and discouraging them from crying or being sad
- Calling people lazy for not hustling during life-altering events like a pandemic
- Minimizing or questioning someone's faith because they are unable to endure suffering or "give their problems to God"
- Telling someone God has a plan for them after a tragedy

We can meet others only as far as we've met ourselves. Often, people who engage in toxic positivity are not intentionally trying to be dismissive of other people's feelings. Most of the time, they themselves are unable to handle their own emotional distress, so it can be difficult for them to be an emotional sounding board for others, especially when the person is exhibiting pain they've spent most of their lives running from.

When we refuse to honor our emotions, we may inadvertently cause harm. As I said earlier, emotions aren't the problem; it's what we do with them that is. But when you decide to ignore your emotional state, you risk acting out in ways that cause conflict and strife in interpersonal relationships. Toxic positivity is not only how we respond to others who are hurting; it can also be how we respond to ourselves.

SELF-IMPOSED TOXIC POSITIVITY LOOKS LIKE:

- Not allowing yourself to feel sad, hurt, or angry because you think it makes you ungrateful for the things going well in your life

- Denying the existence of your pain because you believe other people have it worse
- Pretending to be happy, not to convince others that you are okay, but to convince yourself when you know you aren't
- Thinking that honoring your feelings means giving into your negative emotions
- Thinking that feeling certain emotions makes you weak
- Thinking you will be rewarded for how well you manage your suffering
- Telling yourself that you must be strong, but thinking strength is synonymous with denying the existence of your feelings

Next time you're upset about something, stop saying, "I'm okay," and say this instead:

- "I'm really upset and it's important for me to talk about what happened."
- "I'm having a hard time describing what I'm feeling, but I know I'm not okay."
- "What you did was not okay, and I would like some space to manage my feelings."
- "You've done this before and I didn't speak up then, but now I'm ready to share that your actions have hurt me, and I would like for this to not happen again."
- "I'm not okay right now, and I shut down when I'm overwhelmed by my emotions. Please give me a moment to center myself."

When It Becomes Too Hard to Feel

There are going to be times when your reality is too difficult to process and the emotions tied to your experiences are too heavy to bear. The answer is not to engage in toxic positivity by forcing yourself to feel happy or positive about something extremely tragic; the answer is in building your distress tolerance and finding healthy ways to self-regulate. Sometimes pain is unbearable, and we need to find ways to channel that energy into something that is beneficial for our well-being and that isn't self-destructive.

When I worked with Denise, I learned that she really liked books. I would always find her in the school's library corner browsing different books on the shelf. She mentioned to me that she wished she could write a book one day and that she enjoyed doing things like journaling and writing. The next day in our session, I gave Denise a journal and encouraged her to write the book that was in her heart. She laughed, her face twisted in confusion. "I can't write a book," she responded. I asked her why not, and she gave me a list of reasons why she was unqualified. In return, I explained to Denise that the book was hers. It wasn't about becoming a published author or having a career in writing; it was simply about letting go of the things that take up space in our head and in our hearts. When your heart starts to feel heavy and words are too difficult to utter, write them out. Put words to paper. Tell your story and cherish it as if it were a classic waiting for you in the library on a bookshelf.

Sometimes the pain we feel needs to be released in other ways when we can't untie our tongues and let the pain roll off our lips. For Denise, writing became a coping mechanism when she was emotionally flooded or in emotional distress. It was a healthy escape from her reality that allowed her to practice self-regulation and manage her feelings in a wholesome and nondestructive way.

HEALTHY PRACTICES WHEN DEALING WITH EMOTIONAL DISTRESS:

- **Movement:** Body movement and physical exercise are linked to many benefits for the body, especially for managing your mental health. Movement does not always have to be rigorous, like extreme forms of exercising such as HIIT (high-intensity interval training) or cardio. It can be as simple as stretching daily. Continuous movement and regular exercise can be linked to a decrease in the brain's fight-or-flight response by making them less reactive, which is beneficial for people who struggle with PTSD and anxiety (whether generalized anxiety or social anxiety disorder). If you are new to exercising, consider practices that don't require heavy equipment, such as walking, bike riding, rollerskating, jogging, or even water aerobics. For people with disabilities or limited mobility, walks are helpful, as is yoga, which can be tailored to meet your needs. Other forms of movement, such as cycling and dance, allow you to move at your own pace. The brain and the body are linked, and taking care of your body allows you to take care of your brain.

- **Journaling/Writing:** Sometimes you won't have the ability to talk out your feelings, but writing them out can be just as cathartic. In chapter 1, I shared an exercise for audio journaling. Other outlets can include journaling that focuses on a specific theme, such as intention setting, gratitude, goal setting, and so on. Writing is linked to reducing stress and managing mental health issues such as anxiety and depression. Journaling does not have to be a stringent task; giving yourself five minutes to write can be all you need for the day.

- **Healthy Escapism:** The American Psychological Association defines "escapism" as a tendency to escape from the real world to an alternate fantasy world that feels safe and unthreatening. Escapism is common when dealing with extreme stressors and can be a coping strategy when used in a healthy way. Healthy ways to practice escapism look like swapping your self-help books for fiction, replacing documentaries with comedy shows, gardening and becoming a plant parent, listening to music, journaling, cooking or baking, and even practicing mindfulness. Unhealthy examples of escapism might look like drug, substance, or tobacco use; self-harm; or engaging in unhealthy relationships.

Finding the Right Balance

The goal of distress tolerance is simply to learn how to regulate when in distress. These practices are designed to help you manage intense and difficult emotions; however, they are not meant to be used as avoidance techniques for never addressing your triggers, pain, and trauma. It's imperative that you take the time not only to practice these skills but to address the triggers head-on and not ignore them or act as if they don't exist. We can't fix what we choose to ignore.

"You're Too Old to Be Acting Like That"

When I was working with Denise, I also worked as a trainer providing mental health support and education to the teachers in the school who had to work directly with Denise and her children. About 90 percent of the staff had a great level of antipathy toward Denise, and the hard truth was that in many ways, because of her behavior, Denise indeed came off as an unlikable person. She spoke to people in an ill manner, she yelled and whined when she didn't get her way, she made threats, she cussed and threw tantrums, and she had little regard for how her attitude and actions made people feel. These behaviors were standing in the way of her being able to make connections with others.

What we all must learn to recognize is that if we continue to walk around treating people as if they are the source of our trauma, we will live a lonely life. You can have compassion and empathy for someone who has been harmed and still protect your peace by deciding what you are willing to tolerate from others. The teachers who worked with Denise had decided her behavior was no longer tolerable; however, what they also struggled with was being able to meet Denise where she was. They were expecting something that she could not give. Their argument against her was that she was too old to be acting the way she did, and her childlike behavior was standing in the way of a relationship with her.

Here's a hard truth worth remembering: age does not equal maturity. The people around Denise believed that there was a particular way to act as a twenty-year-old, and she was not meeting their expectations. We've been conditioned to believe that with age comes wisdom, when the reality is that wisdom is learned, and if we are not doing the work to educate ourselves and garner the skills needed to mature, then we will continue to lack wisdom, regardless of how old we are.

Age does not equal maturity.

Working with Denise, in many ways, was like working with a child. She was constantly in a state of fight or flight, causing her to become emotionally dysregulated whenever things happened outside her window of control, which led to emotionally immature behaviors. And as a result, her behavior harmed not only her but the people she so desperately wanted to be around.

EMOTIONAL IMMATURITY LOOKS LIKE:

- Getting defensive in response to difficult conversations or being challenged—especially when you are being challenged for the harm you caused
- Engaging in impulsive (sometimes destructive) behaviors
- Blaming others for your mistakes instead of taking responsibility

- Throwing tantrums and lashing out when you feel difficult emotions
- Making other people responsible for fixing your feelings
- Being unable to plan or commit to plans, people, or responsibilities
- Being unable to hear the needs of others
- Having a lack of desire to change or problem-solve
- Expecting others to adjust, while making no effort to compromise
- Having a lack of self-awareness and personal agency

Being emotionally immature impacts our ability to be resilient and handle conflict in a healthy way. It also affects our ability to form healthy interpersonal relationships. People who are emotionally immature have a hard time seeing things beyond themselves. They are focused on their own feelings and emotions and have little regard for the feelings and emotions of others. They are also quick to criticize others for their actions and wrongdoings but refuse to hold themselves accountable for their own actions that cause others harm as well. In my household growing up, when I had my moments of being pompous, I heard these words from my parents all the time: "You can dish it out, but you can't take it." Which means, in other words, you have no problem treating people with contempt, but hate for that contempt to come full circle.

Emotional maturity is developed through learning emotional intelligence—which is our ability to perceive, process, regulate, and manage our emotions in a healthy manner. Denise was often very reactive because she believed everyone was out to get her. She had experienced so much hurt in life that she struggled with differentiating between harm and support. Denise was almost always in fight mode, and it was for the sake of her survival. The first step to helping Denise restore her trigger responses was for her to tap into self-awareness and be in tune with her body more. When we feel emotions, we often feel sensations in the body accompanying them. Deepening your connection to your body can allow you to see where you are holding tension and stress or when your nervous system is dysregulated.

BODY AWARENESS INCLUDES NOTICING:

- Tightness in the chest
- Difficulty breathing
- Jumpy movements: leg shaking, jerkiness, etc.
- Sweating: the face, under the arms, clammy hands, etc.
- Nail biting or bodily harm: pinching yourself, pulling your hair out, scratching to the point of leaving scars
- Tensed muscles
- Gut imbalance: upset stomach, knots in stomach, etc.

By becoming more in tune with her body, Denise was able to notice when she was starting to feel triggered, and this awareness helped her choose better behaviors that weren't harmful. This also helped her with learning the power of pause. Because Denise was so used to being reactive, she had to learn how to become more mindful and present in the moment.

Mindfulness helps us tap into our emotional state, and when we realize we are off-balance, we can learn to pause and disengage from the thing that feels like a threat. Being one with her body helped her to become more mindful of her triggers and how they manifested in her. And with this tool, Denise was able to reflect on how her next steps would impact her. Self-awareness helps us to be mindful of our choices. People who are emotionally immature tend to blame others for their mishaps instead of taking ownership of their decisions. Self-awareness allows people to see how they have ownership of their own choices, and because of that, whatever consequences that come because of those choices are a debt that they themselves must pay.

When Denise became more self-aware, she stopped behaving so impulsively.

BUILDING EMOTIONAL MATURITY LOOKS LIKE:

- Learning to identify and name what you feel instead of pretending not to care or be unbothered by things
- Learning to manage your uncomfortable feelings instead of letting your feelings control you
- Learning to be an active listener with the intent to understand (and not judge, defend, or deflect)
- Expressing your emotions in a healthy and respectful manner
- Thinking before you react
- Paying attention to triggers and the body's warning signs
- Feeling your emotions without judgment or shame
- Investigating the cause of your emotions

- Learning to take ownership of your choices and stop blaming people for your actions

What We Leave Behind

My work with Denise was one of the hardest cases I have ever had. Her exterior was difficult, complicated, and stubborn, but on the inside, she was caring and loving, and she deeply yearned to be loved and cared for in return. A few months after I had completed my work with Denise, she passed away due to natural causes. Despite all the limitations she had—a lack of support, unhealed trauma, and more—she made a choice one day to heal not just for herself but for her children. She made a choice to sit with her pain and open herself up to a stranger about the life she lived and the things that tormented her. No matter what she was going through, she showed up to that school building every single day, because that place was her home—it's where she found community.

Death Is the Only Finish Line

There is no arrival. Our arrival comes when we are greeted by death. As long as we are alive, healing will be an everyday practice, which also means that there is no perfect start time. Healing does not have an expiration date or an age requirement. It is never too late to get started on the life you desire. And it's never too late to give yourself the life you think you deserve. You may not have control over everything, but it's up to you to

It is never too late to heal from your trauma.

define your future and make a choice to do better for the person you want to be tomorrow, and for the person you want to be ten years from now. It is never too late to heal from your trauma. It is never too late to get up and try one more time. Healing is a sacred act that is strictly reserved for the living. We have the power and the choice to lean into the intricacies of our humanity to build resilience and persevere. I know you are probably tired of having to be resilient. I know you are tired of adversity and hardship. I'm sorry; I wish I could make you a promise that only good things are ahead of you, but I cannot. We do not know what tomorrow brings, but we can choose to stand tall and make today meaningful. Sometimes we don't live long enough to see the fruits of our labor, but I promise that planting the seed is also good enough. Starting now is good enough. I hope Denise's children can see the seeds she planted—the seeds of hope, courage, and endurance—and I also hope that one day they get to pick the fruits of her love and labor.

Exercise: Writing Reflections

- Your choice to heal will leave a legacy. What legacy do you want your healing to leave behind?

- In what ways have you harmed others as a result of living in trauma? What are you doing to hold yourself accountable moving forward?
- In your opinion, what does maturity look like? Do you see yourself embodying these traits daily? What can you improve upon if not?
- Body scan: What signs do you notice in your body when you are becoming dysregulated? What practices from this chapter will you start doing as a coping skill?

— 3 —

THE STRUGGLE FOR SAFE SPACES

Cultivating Wellness in a World Full of Racism

Being Black Isn't Exhausting, White Supremacy Is

When I was ten years old, while on vacation in Fort Myers, Florida, I was walking through a Home Depot one afternoon with my uncle, who is deaf, while my parents navigated a different part of the store. As I shopped with my uncle, two white male police officers began approaching us. We were the only two people in the aisle, and as they got closer, I immediately felt frozen in my body from how hard their glares were and the direct eye contact they made with me. At the time, the most I knew about the police was that interacting with one meant that you had done something bad, and from the way their eyes were set on me, I started feeling guilty for just breathing, even though I knew I had done nothing wrong.

When they approached me, one of the officers said, "Ma'am, I need to see your ID." When his words hit my ears, I wondered for a second if this was a cruel joke. Maybe a prank of some kind. I had always been mistaken for being older, I guess because I was tall for my age, but I had never been called "ma'am" before, nor had anyone ever thought I was old enough to be walking around with identification. I was so much at a loss for words that I just stared at him, right into his dark, glassy eyes, while he stood above me with his hands on his hips waiting for me to follow his orders. My expression was clearly perplexed, and that is when the other officer stepped in and asked, "How old are you, young lady?" I responded with cracks in my voice, "I'm ten." My uncle was standing right beside me the whole time, waiting for me to sign to him what was going on, and he looked just as perplexed as I did. The officer began to turn to my uncle, but I quickly interjected and explained that he was deaf and wouldn't be able to communicate. They asked me if my parents were in the store, and at that moment, I sent my uncle to go find them as I waited behind.

In retrospect, now that I am an adult, I think about this moment often because it is so deeply etched in my memory. I think about how these officers had no regard for my uncle, who was the adult, as they approached me, a child, despite mistaking me for being older; they did not care about his presence or that I was possibly a minor. What I also think about is the decision that I made to be left alone with them as I sent my uncle to find my parents. Ten-year-old me was paralyzed with fear, and when they made a case for needing to speak to my parents, I felt more fear for what they possibly thought I had done.

When my parents arrived, I could see concern sketched in their faces as they approached me while I stood there in between two white male cops. My parents asked what they wanted, and the first officer who addressed me shared that a woman in the store reported that I had stolen her purse and taken her wallet. I couldn't believe what I was hearing, and neither could my parents. Five minutes prior I had been too afraid to utter a word, but after hearing this false claim, my voice came back to me. I started shouting that they had the wrong person, that I hadn't done anything of that nature. I even started giving an alibi, stating that I was with my uncle the whole time and I had a key witness. The officers, however, didn't seem to believe me, saying that the woman didn't appear to be lying and that she was also very afraid and terrified for her life. And it was at that moment that both of my parents lost it, and their calm demeanor turned agitated as they raised their voices. I stood back in silence, allowing my parents to defend me, and I heard them say, "This is because we're Black, isn't it?" And I could see the manifestation of a righteous anger ignite inside them as they continued on exclaiming that we were being harassed for being Black, by both of them and some woman who refused to reveal her identity. At no point did the officers ever involve store management. They never requested to see camera footage. They never inquired whether there were witnesses. Whoever this woman was, she was being protected, while I had to endure the harm of being falsely accused of a crime I did not commit.

I don't know what changed their minds, but the more my parents defended me and refused to back down, the more the two officers seemed to become less interested in pursuing me as a suspect. Which is when the second officer said to my parents that maybe they had the wrong person, so they were going to "let me go," as if they were doing me a favor and giving me a pass.

In the car ride home, my parents never stopped talking about the interaction, and I couldn't shake their words from my head: "It's because we're Black." Prior to that incident, I had never thought about the color of my skin and what it meant for me when it came to navigating life and my interactions with people. I was very curious as to why my parents had brought up race, and when we got home that night, they had to explain to ten-year-old me that, for as long as I'm alive, I would deal with things due to the color of my skin. People would have their minds made up about who I am. They would accuse me of crimes. That I would be judged and that I would have to work twice as hard to prove myself to folks who don't look like me, all because I was Black. And when I replayed in my head what happened with those police officers, I understood my parents' fear and concern. I know I was only ten, but by then I already had a great deal of emotional maturity, and I knew something about that interaction was unclear. How nonchalantly they accused me, as well as how easily they decided to leave the situation alone. Since when do the police just walk away from a crime with no real investigation into what happened? It was the mysterious woman's word against mine, and I knew my parents were thinking that it was this woman's word against a Black child's.

From that day forward, I became highly cognizant of my race, something that I had never given much thought to before. I grew up in a predominantly Black neighborhood and went to a predominantly Black school. On weekends my parents would frequent places like Flatbush, Brooklyn, or Jamaica Avenue, Queens, where we came across other Caribbean people with heavy accents and a shared language from back home where my parents are from. On days when my dad wanted to a buy a new record, we'd head into Jackson Heights to visit his favorite music store, and then we'd have dinner at his favorite Colombian restaurant, where my parents spoke Spanish and we'd feast on rice and beans, chicharrónes, tostones, pernil, and other dishes that were familiar to my parents' homelands in both Panama and San Andrés, Colombia. I grew up proud of my heritage, my culture, and my race, and that day in Home Depot changed everything about how I saw myself and moved through the world.

When I think about that police officer who addressed me as "ma'am," I think about the many ways innocence is ripped off Black children like old clothes clinging loosely to our bodies. Language matters, and the use of this word implied that he did not have to treat me like a child if it came down to it—if things were to escalate, if force needed to be used, I would've faced adultlike consequences, both mentally and physically, without a second of doubt. I carried the weight of that encounter for the rest of my childhood and adolescent years, and it even made me hate certain aspects of myself and my developing body. At that age I had already gotten my period, which started when I was nine years old. Other kids in the class found out after I had an accident that required a change of clothes, and when I learned no one else's body was changing, bleeding, and cramping like mine, it made me feel like something was wrong with me—I felt like less of a child. So by the time I was ten, I was already very self-conscious, especially since I was at a solid height of five foot seven.

Everywhere I went, people presumed I was much older, and I watched how my teachers interacted with me compared to other kids in the class who were shorter, lighter skinned, and with baby-like faces and who, when standing next to me, looked like my little siblings despite us being the same age.

Adultification bias is when people in authoritative roles, such as teachers, law enforcement, and even parents, perceive young Black children as much older than they are, almost adultlike, which causes them to treat these children more punitively, by withholding care, nurturing, and even safety and protection. In 2017, the Georgetown Law Center on Poverty and Inequality did a research study titled *Girlhood Interrupted: The Erasure of Black Girls' Childhood*, which shed light on the adultification bias young Black girls and boys face compared to their white peers. In their research, it was revealed through a study done by Professor Phillip Goff that, from the age of ten, Black boys are perceived as older and more likely to be guilty than their white peers and that police violence against them is more justified. Seasoned police officers who were also sampled in the study consistently overestimated the age of Black adolescent felony suspects by approximately 4.5 years. White suspects, however, were perceived as younger than their actual age.

When it comes to Black girls, the study revealed that adults view them as less innocent and more adultlike compared to their white peers, primarily in the age range of five to fourteen. Teachers shared reports of perceiving them as loud, very mature, controlling, and even threatening, which isn't surprising seeing how Black women are perceived through the same lens. It's as if our innocence is seen as something we are supposed to earn by falling in line, keeping our mouths shut, and tolerating any kind of behavior—even when it's harmful or abusive—or else we will face harsh penalties for simply existing.

I may not be a mother, but I have the responsibility of mothering my young nieces, nephews, and godchildren. Community-care requires us to show up for those who are most vulnerable to systems of oppression and have a greater likelihood of dealing with social inequities. Mothering has many facets, but at its core is nurturing and caring for our young ones— even when these young ones are not biologically our own.

When I think about my teenage nephew, a young Black boy with a trauma history and an ADHD (attention deficit hyperactivity disorder) diagnosis, I worry about the repercussions he will face for having a neurodivergent brain that causes him to behave differently in social spaces— whether that be in school or in public. I've had to have countless conversations with him about how to handle police interactions if he were ever to find himself face-to-face with a cop the same way I did when I was only ten. My encounters with the police did not stop at age ten, however; they have gone on into adulthood. As a Black woman, I am almost always pulled over by white police officers, which puts me in a state of hyperarousal, a symptom of PTSD that manifests as fight or flight, which looks like anxiety, panic attacks, rage, hypervigilance, difficulty concentrating, and so on.

I will never forget being pulled over by a cop who berated me for going two miles over the speed limit. I was doing thirty-two miles per hour in a thirty zone. He would not stop screaming and cussing the air all while I kept my hands on the steering wheel, watching his movements, hoping and praying his hands would not reach for his gun, as I saw how provoked and dysregulated he was. My niece, who was only three at the time, was in the backseat. It was just us two, which meant a sufficient witness was not present to tell my side of the story if I would have ended up dead from that encounter. I had never pleaded for a cop to give me a ticket before, but this time I did, and that made him angrier. He took my documents, and I watched him walk to his car as he continued to yell and scream, but he never got inside. Instead, he turned back toward my car, handed me my documents, and told me to drive safely because I had a child in the car. My own panic and freeze responses have shown me that talking to my nieces about the police is no different than talking to my nephews. Being in a Black body puts you at risk for being a target for someone who holds both racial bias and willful ignorance.

In 2020, many of us witnessed the truth of this when George Floyd was murdered in broad daylight by a police officer. The aftermath of this act of violence set off a long chain of events, and suddenly many people started opening their eyes to the racism Black people had already been shouting still exists. What struck me the most, however, is this narrative that started to circulate on social media stemming from a tweet that read "Being Black is exhausting." Reading these words filled me with grief. It made me sad to know that someone had felt this so heavily, and my emotions felt tangled up in a knot that I kept trying to pick apart because I had questioned whether I, too, shared the same sentiments and experienced the same level of exhaustion. I was indeed exhausted, but my exhaustion had nothing to do with being in Black skin; it had everything to do with the power of white supremacy and how its roots run deep within American soil.

The belief that whiteness is superior is deeply ingrained in the minds of many white people (and people of color, but we'll unpack internalized racism later), and it shows up through both overt and covert acts of violence, harm, abuse, and power hoarding on both a micro and a macro level. White supremacy manifests when Black children face adultification bias, which then leads to the school-to-prison pipeline, which then leads to the criminal justice system. White supremacy manifests when white people act as authority figures, demanding to see proof of identification when Black people are trying to enter their privately owned homes, neighborhoods, and apartment buildings. White supremacy manifests when white cops decide to kill Black children because their racial bias classifies Black boys as thugs and girls as ghetto. I am not exhausted by being in my Black skin; I am exhausted by the world of ignorance and hatred that swirls around me. I am exhausted by the justification of killing people who do not fall in line with tyrannical authority. I am very much exhausted by systems of oppression that have roots in slavery. What's most tiring is the struggle for safe spaces. Anywhere in the world can be a threat to Black people, including simple day-to-day spaces like the grocery store, work, school, the park, a restaurant, and even a doctor's office.

BEING BLACK ISN'T EXHAUSTING

- White supremacy is exhausting
- Systemic racism is exhausting
- White feminism is exhausting
- Race-based violence is exhausting
- Oppression is exhausting
- Injustice is exhausting

When we learn to redirect our energy toward the oppressor, we see that we have been involuntarily thrown into a wrestling ring and forced to fight for our freedom, safety, and livelihoods, all because our opponent refuses to honor us as human beings. Instead, our opponent—who is anyone who still carries a white supremacy mindset (and this even goes for those who are BIPOC themselves)—is the one who's exhausting us, not our Blackness or our culture. I've rejected the idea that being Black is exhausting because if I see myself, a Black woman, as America's problem, then what is the solution? Where do we as a people and nation go from here?

I remember a conversation with a good friend of mine who is white. She asked me how I comfortably move through the world knowing that all this hate about who I am exists around me. How do I make peace with that? How am I not always angry but often full of joy? I responded by telling her that I am very much aware that there are people in this world who hate me for being Black, but I love myself, and how I see myself trumps the opinions of others. I cannot allow the judgments of others to rule and define how I live my life.

Does it suck that there will be places in this world that I am not welcomed or invited to simply for my race? Or that a person would dislike me simply for my race? Of course, but I know exactly what I deserve, and I will never let a racist person make me feel bad about existing. Never. I make a conscious choice every single day to live in alignment with what I deserve and surround myself with people who deserve to have access to me. I will never shrink myself, play small, or stop speaking up because I am concerned about being cast as a stereotype. If a person thinks I'm an angry Black woman for having an opinion, they must deal with that.

I am not responsible for managing other people's racist judgments about me. I am exhausted enough by the weight of the world and all the things I already must carry, so I refuse to do someone else's antiracism work.

Whether you are Black or a person of color, you must make a cognizant choice, every single day, about what narratives you are willing to accept and reject when it comes to owning who you are and being firmly planted in your identity. When I work with BIPOC on mental health in the workplace, I often get asked, "How do I speak up without the fear of being labeled or stereotyped?" And if you ever had this concern, I invite you to do an exercise where you reframe your language.

Original thought: "How do I do x *without* the fear of . . ."

Reframed thought: "How do I do x *despite* the fear of . . ."

Here's the hard truth. You are a person with feelings and emotions, and your actions will land on a person who has feelings and emotions as well. We are not emotionless people. You do yourself a disservice when you hold off speaking up because you are trying to be fearless. Instead of saying, "How can I do this thing without fear?" you must teach yourself that fear does not rule you or control you and you can honor that you feel afraid while you simultaneously seek justice and stand up for yourself. It *is* scary—after all, BIPOC know firsthand that people are always ready to punish us for doing what they consider stepping out of line—but what we also must remember is that often our fears are rooted in assumptions, and our assumptions hold us back from taking action. I can assume a person will criticize me and turn me into a stereotype, or I can make the decision to speak up and do that hard thing and give people an opportunity to show me who they are. When they do, I can hold on to that knowledge of them to give me clarity on whether they are safe and how to do life with them.

Trying to live a fearless life in a world where threats can be constant isn't always practical. Our former great leaders and changemakers, like Dr. Martin Luther King Jr., Dr. Dorothy Height, Harriet Tubman, and Rosa Parks, or even current ones, like the Obamas, Alexandria Ocasio-Cortez, or Malala Yousafzai, knew their commitment to change would cost them something, and that is a scary thing to have to digest and reconcile, but when you know you are going to suffer either way, you make a choice to liberate yourself and own that the fight is greater than the consequence.

Reflect here: What are the things that you have been afraid to do that you know need to get done? Fill in the empty bullet points below. (You can also do this in a journal.)

Despite feeling fear, I have the power to:

- Speak up and express my boundaries both in my personal life and in the workplace
- Make changes in my life to advance and excel
- Meet the goals that I set for myself
- Change policies and practices in the workplace to better enhance workplace well-being
- Say no the to things I do not want to do
-
-
-

Internalized Oppression and the White Gaze

When I first started attending graduate school at NYU, it felt like race-based culture shock. Growing up in a predominantly Black and Brown community meant I was always surrounded by people who looked like me, especially in school. Even my undergraduate program was diverse, but the social work program at NYU was far from diverse on both a student and a staff level, which both triggered and awakened different parts of me that I wasn't aware needed healing.

As a child, I was made fun of for how I spoke at times. My parents are of Panamanian and Colombian (San Andrés region) descent, so they spoke San Andrés Creole, an English-based creole influenced by West Africa. Outside of that, my parents' secondary language was Spanish, so naturally there were some English words they would misspell or mispronounce, but because I picked up English at home, I did not realize the words they spoke at times needed correction. In school, I'd repeat the words I heard my parents say, and kids would snicker, causing an eruption of giggles in the classroom. "What did you just say?" they would ask, and I would repeat myself until I began to realize they had heard what I said—it was just that *how* I said it was funny to their ears, which caused me to shrink myself into silence to avoid the constant embarrassment that I felt.

I started to feel ashamed of my nationality and wished my parents would speak the way Americans spoke, even though they aren't American. I carried this internalized hatred with me for a long time until I started to learn how to play dress-up with different personality traits. I could be two different people all while living in the same body. My favorite TV shows as a teen were *Girlfriends* and *Sex and the City*. I couldn't see myself in Carrie Bradshaw, but as a native New Yorker I wanted to be her, and so as I navigated places in Manhattan like Chelsea and the West Village for school, I thought about who Joan from *Girlfriends* would be if she was living in NYC and attending NYU, walking around campus, meeting new people, and engaging with this part of the city I had never frequented before my admission to grad school. It was a chance for me to be someone I was not, but the issue was that Joan, too, was a Black woman, and when you are constantly in the gaze of white people, it can be hard to wonder whether your Blackness is a distraction from the other unique elements of yourself, such as your character, personality, intelligence, and other things that make up who we are as individuals.

Because I was so hyperfixated on how I spoke and afraid of embarrassing myself, I tended to be very quiet, which always made people think I was shy and introverted. In class, I would barely raise my hand to participate. What I was battling was something called internalized oppression—I didn't feel good enough, or smart, because I felt my vocabulary was lacking and my way of talking would be deemed as hood, ghetto, or uneducated. The question is by whom—it was by white people, because I have to be honest and admit that I couldn't have cared less about how Black and Brown people viewed me or what they thought of me, and that realization made me have to adjust to the fact that I was performing for the white gaze. I had unfortunately come to learn that I was struggling with an inferiority complex and had this inherited belief that whiteness was indeed superior, and I had to talk, walk, and act like them to reach the pinnacle of success. I wanted to be Joan Clayton, but deep down I was aiming to be more like Carrie Bradshaw—consistently molding and reshaping myself, finding ways to see how I could lean more into whiteness.

When a marginalized group faces discrimination and racism and experiences acts of hatred over a long period of time, they can begin to believe the oppressive ideologies that have been placed on them the more they experience trauma or racial violence. The outward hate they face now becomes inward hate. People who struggle with internalized oppression may not feel it only in the effects of race; it can also impact women, people with disabilities, people living in poverty, immigrants, and others.

For me, being Black-Hispanic, a woman, and the child of immigrants made me feel like I had to jump through many hoops to be seen, heard, and valued. I was trying to prove that people like me were worthy, but instead of owning that myself, I was parading around like someone I was not, trying to gain proximity to whiteness and shrinking myself all so that I wouldn't be placed in a box, created without my consent, that was filled with oppressive stereotypes and dehumanizing ideologies about who I am and what I was capable of being. However, what's unfortunate about harboring internalized oppression is that the oppressed individual begins to create those boxes they fought so hard to not be placed in. It starts off with you hating parts of yourself; then it magnifies into you hating others who look just like you and share the same lived experiences, because inward hate eventually turns outward. It becomes loud and obnoxious, and it manifests itself through the slightest actions of judgment and projection.

Trauma and Its Burden on the Body for BIPOC

Exploring the roots of internalized oppression requires us to learn how America's history with race has influenced our self-esteem and perception of self. Historical trauma refers to when a cultural, racial, or ethnic group of people experience cumulative acts of harm and violence over a lengthy period—which leaves behind generations of people struggling with PTSD. For a very long time, we have viewed PTSD through the lens of war and veterans without considering how slavery—an act of war against and dehumanization of Black and Brown people—has caused bodily and mental harm. (Similar harms have also been caused by forced migration, the colonization of Native Americans, and other historical events that have been violent toward racial groups and cultures.) A lot of folks believe that because we are four hundred years removed from chattel slavery, the trauma of slavery in no way, shape, or form can still exist. So to give it greater context, let's unpack a more recent traumatic event—for example, the attack on the World Trade Center on September 11, 2001. Now, although we are not four hundred years removed from this tragic event in history, studies show that twenty years later, people who were in the area, as well as those who witnessed the disaster, are struggling with PTSD to this day. Robert Brackbill, director of research at the World Trade Health Center Registry, reported to NPR: "Each time we do a survey, it's between 8% and 10% that have sufficient symptoms to indicate post-traumatic stress disorder. But among people who had a closer experience of the disaster, such as occupants of the building, or rescue and recovery workers, the rates are even higher—about 17% to 18%." As a result of 9/11, many people walked away not just with mental health issues but chronic health conditions and illnesses, from asthma to cancer. This is a reminder that trauma stores itself in the body, and releasing it can require a lifetime of work, treatment, and healing.

Trauma stores itself in the body.

Imagine living in a time loop and waking up every single day experiencing 9/11 all over again—for four hundred years. This one event has left a legacy of pain, hurt, and PTSD, yet it seems so hard for some to understand how being brutally harmed, beaten, and enslaved for four hundred years can leave a long-lasting mental and emotional impact on the generations that have followed.

In 1865 when American slavery was abolished, there was no trauma-informed care; there were no mental health clinics and treatment centers for the living victims of violence and abuse; there weren't even any reparations of any kind to aid Black and Brown people financially, physically, mentally, or emotionally.

Black people were now free but had no proper education, guidance, or life skills on how to integrate into a free society. These people who were once enslaved knew of only one life, because they came from a tortured history. There was no past to reminisce about because their parents, grandparents, and even great-grandparents were all most likely enslaved and all hoped that one day they would see freedom. Now here freedom was, but how do you hold it in your hands when it feels so heavy? People who were enslaved would most likely meet the criteria for PTSD, and when trauma is untreated, it doesn't impact only you—it impacts your children as well as your community.

As adults, we are shaped by the experiences we endured during childhood, and if those experiences are not managed or treated, we run the risk of reenacting them in our interpersonal relationships. So when you are enslaved and now become free, what do you teach your children about what it means to be human in America? To be Black, to be loved, to be cared for, to belong, when you yourself are possibly still searching for those answers? We learn to raise our children based on how we were raised. In some cases, we can learn skills and tools from our environment and other nurturing and safe relationships to help us make different choices, but that is not an experience everyone has as they enter the role of parenting. This isn't to say that people who were enslaved did not know how to take care of their children; however, we must acknowledge the impact that our lived experiences have on our beliefs, values, and ideologies about ourselves and the world around us, as well as how we manage distressing situations and respond to difficult life events. So although we are four hundred years removed from chattel slavery, we are not that far removed from the mental and emotional effects of slavery that were passed down through generations.

Learning to break intergenerational trauma requires us to examine the many ways our family unit has been broken and how we've internalized the oppressors' tactics to keep us in a state of mental destruction and self-oppression. Issues such as colorism, spankings, and even extreme impostor syndrome and self-doubt are all examples of PTSD that has been passed down through our ancestors' untreated traumas. Now in our current society, a lot of us are holding on to oppression under the guise of family traditions or naming something as a form of culture.

Whenever I talk about boundaries, one of the common responses I receive is: "This would never be okay in my X [insert Black, Hispanic,

South/East Asian, etc.] household." The oppressed have been told for a very long time that they are not allowed to have a voice, and internalized oppression tells us that we are not allowed to speak up. A lot of us are inadvertently clinging to narratives that we are not allowed to be fully human—a narrative that masters on the plantation carried toward those who were enslaved. Some of us have become so bonded to trauma that we are conflating disrespect with tradition, and then teaching this to our children. If the traditions we are upholding in our family units are abuse tactics that are being used to silence others or take away their agency, then we are moving further away from community and deeper into dysfunction.

Treating internalized oppression also allows us to repair both our community and the family unit, which suffer because of intergenerational, institutional, and systemic trauma. This is where we start to recognize that self-care is the bridge to community-care, and community-care is the bridge to community healing. When we care for ourselves by challenging our own oppressive ideologies, we are simultaneously caring for others by engaging less in harmful behaviors, challenging our biases, and allowing others to take up space without the fear that our voices will be silenced if we pass the mic.

**INDIVIDUALIZED INTERNALIZED OPPRESSION
CAN MANIFEST AS:**

- Women avoiding leadership roles out of fear that they will be judged and perceived negatively as problematic, etc.
- Women, particularly BIPOC women, experiencing impostor

syndrome as a result of seeing success portrayed in a particular way (white, male, cis), which causes them to discredit their qualifications, skills, and knowledge; feel the need to work harder than others; and set unrealistic standards or feel like a fraud and not deserving to exist in certain spaces

- Immigrants or first-gen children feeling ashamed of having an accent or how they speak the English language

INTERNALIZED OPPRESSION WITHIN SAME CULTURAL GROUPS CAN MANIFEST AS:

- BIPOC individuals desiring to date or be in proximity only with people who are light-skinned or white because they believe people of their same cultural group who are dark-skinned are not beautiful or handsome, or are inferior, criminals, lacking intelligence, etc.
- BIPOC individuals believing only white people should be in leadership roles specifically because of their race and not because of their ability to be great leaders
- BIPOC telling other BIPOC they are talking like a white person because of their vocabulary

Understanding the ways internalized oppression manifests in our day-to-day lives helps us understand the way we show up for ourselves and our communities. When we shrink ourselves and hold degrading beliefs about who we are as individuals, it impacts how we move through the world and engage in relationships. If we want to tackle injustices and create safe healing spaces, we, too, must be willing to look inward and assess the ideologies that we believe in that might be holding us back from collective change. Supporting our communities requires that we be introspective and examine the burdens that we bring to our communities and place on each other's backs.

As a first-gen Panamanian woman who once idolized whiteness, I've learned that the beliefs that I once held did nothing to further my community and instead only created more of a divide. I also learned that the more I oppressed myself, the more I missed out on opportunities to be in roles that would have allowed me to create change and empower other folks from the same cultural group as me, as well as others who are marginalized and oppressed. By oppressing myself, I handed over my power to others who were already benefiting from their own inherited power created by white supremacy. We need to be empowered to heal and fight against inequality and inequities, but if we are constantly holding on to self-doubt, impostor syndrome, and negative stereotypes of who we are, then the power we hold will be misused, and instead of cultivating change, we may induce more harm.

The good news is that there are ways to heal the internalized oppression that we carry, but this is not a one-time fix; it will require a lifetime of work and commitment to learning and unlearning. As BIPOC, we must first examine the ways we've been programmed to see ourselves and push against narratives that are dehumanizing, and this starts in the home. It's common for internalized oppression to be deeply rooted in family ideologies, due to the experiences our ancestors had and America's history—from slavery all the way to Jim Crow and the negative ways we are consistently portrayed in the media.

REFLECTIONS TO COME BACK TO:

- What did your parents teach you about your culture? Did they embrace things like their accent, language, etc., or did they harbor shame and scrutiny about how they spoke?

- What did your parents teach you about the color of your skin as a BIPOC individual? Did they make negative comments about you or others being darker-skinned? Did they praise people for being light-skinned? Did they teach you how to love your shade and what it means to be beautiful or handsome? Did they believe being fair-skinned gave them proximity to whiteness?

- What messages did you hear in your household about success? How did your parents push you to excel and help you see your worth, value, and skills? How did they encourage you and teach you that you had the ability to be successful despite your race, class, or gender? What did that encouragement look like?

- What messages did you hear (and see played out) in your household regarding gender roles? Did you see an imbalance in household or caregiving responsibilities based solely on the idea that men and women had assigned roles to play in the home? Were you raised to believe that because of your gender, you had to act and behave in a specific way (e.g., men don't cry or show emotions; men work outside the home, not within the home; women must cook and clean and never be angry; women must be submissive, etc.)? How has this impacted you and the relationships you form as an adult? How has this impacted your ability to own and process your emotions?

- Growing up, and even now as an adult, did you see yourself depicted positively in the media, from cartoons to TV shows? What did entertainment and media teach you about your cultural identity? Were there family-oriented shows that had cast members who looked like you and held you up in a positive regard? Did you have dolls or toys that resembled you? Were you taught certain toys, specifically white dolls, for example, were better and prettier than Black dolls? How did this impact your self-esteem and sense of self?

Reaffirming your worth and seeing the value in your cultural group and identity are necessities in being able to manage your self-esteem and self-worth. This looks like engaging in positive self-talk, while also refusing to participate in conversations with others that are demeaning and degrading to people of other groups and cultures, as well as to your own. We all deserve to live a full life, and as individuals, we all deserve to be treated with respect. When we fight against internalized oppression, we are building up our communities and transforming how we see ourselves in this world.

Being Superwoman:
Healing from the Strong Black Woman Trope

Doing the work of fighting injustice and facing adversity requires both strength and perseverance; however, there are moments when we can overidentify with the need to be strong all the time to the point where it becomes a detriment to our mental health, leaving us impaired and emotionally injured. I remember hitting a point in my life when I would wake up and feel as if getting suited for battle was a part of my morning routine. The first time I began forcing myself to exhibit strength was twenty-four hours after my father died, when I was nineteen years old. His death brought forth a lot of additional responsibilities that I was not equipped to handle, but whether I was ready or not, things had to get done and I needed to adapt quickly or else I would crumble. This caused me to suppress my grief, so I stuffed all my emotions into a box, duct-taped it shut, and labeled it as "to be dealt with eventually." Well, every time "eventually" came, I kept stuffing my emotions right back into that box because I was scared confronting them would cripple me. All I kept thinking was, "I need to remain strong; I can't deal with this right now."

And so that is what I did. I kept moving forward in life, suited up in my armor and ready to take on all the world would throw at me with a brave smile. I prided myself on being independent, not succumbing to my emotions, and feeling as if I didn't need anyone—not their help, handouts, or favors. These qualities of mine earned me the nickname the "Strong Friend," and when other people felt like their yoke was too heavy a burden to carry, they would lay it at my feet as if I were Jesus and had the miraculous powers to heal. I became all-knowing in the eyes of many friends, peers, and even colleagues, because I was very outspoken in the workplace. I was the person you ran to with problems you needed to dump and sort through. At the time, I had thought this gave my life purpose in some way—to be able to help others and show up consistently without any boundaries—but the more I was this person, the more I found myself grieving and growing irritable and snappy. I was secretly yearning for my former life, the one I had before my father died when I wasn't everyone's sanctuary. Instead, I had had my own sanctuary where I could lay my burdens down. I knew I needed help, but I had become so enmeshed with being known as the "Strong Friend" that I wasn't sure who I would be to others, or even to myself, if I admitted that I felt weak and wanted to cling to that weakness just so that I could feel something again.

My overidentification with being strong felt like something I had not chosen. Instead, it felt forced on me, as if I didn't have an option to be anything else but strong, because to survive in this world, especially as a Black woman, I always needed to be two steps ahead. From young, I had been warned that being in my skin would always come with challenges. Ten-year-old me, who was close to being arrested for a crime that I did not commit, was already being taught how to mentally prepare myself for simply walking out the door of my home into a world full of opposition as well as threats to my race and gender. Meanwhile, while I was living at home, my mother was instilling in me the importance of being self-sufficient, independent, and untrusting of others—which stemmed from her own trauma that shaped her flawed perception of interdependence and made her fearful of leaning on community. These messages I heard were intended to be empowering, but instead, they were burdensome, leading me to feel afraid or like a failure for needing help, wanting support, and not wanting to be depended on all the time and seen as a person and not a savior.

MYTHS ABOUT WHAT IT MEANS TO BE STRONG

- Pretending to have it all together when you don't
- Presenting yourself as perfect over being human
- Suppressing your emotions and lacking vulnerability
- Putting other people's needs before your own
- Fixing and saving other people from their problems
- Pretending to be unaffected by adversity and pushing through without complaints
- Having tough skin and dealing with problematic behaviors instead of setting boundaries

WHAT IT REALLY LOOKS LIKE TO BE STRONG

- Admitting when you don't know something
- Admitting that you need help and asking for it
- Allowing yourself to feel all your emotions, not just the good ones
- Allowing yourself to cry if you need to
- Pushing through adversity while simultaneously acknowledging the hurt that comes with it
- Being vulnerable and learning to trust others

The more we subscribe to these myths about what it means to be strong, the more we will face difficulties and challenges when it comes to growing and having a healthy relationship with ourselves and others. In many cases, what we view as strength on the surface can be a form of counterdependency at the root of our actions. At the root of every healthy relationship is intimacy. Many people are familiar with the word "intimacy" only in the context of sex; however, we can have four main types of intimacy within our interpersonal relationships.

At the root of every healthy relationship is intimacy.

Emotional Intimacy: A sense of safety related to the expression of thoughts and feelings. Includes feelings of empathy and compassion versus shame or judgment.

Intellectual Intimacy: The sharing of beliefs, viewpoints, opinions, and perspectives that allows people to be vulnerable with their truths and creates a sense of closeness, relatability, and connection.

Experiential Intimacy: The sharing of experiences and memories that creates bonds and closer levels of connection.

Physical/Sexual Intimacy: The sharing of passion, pleasure, and closeness through physical touch or sexual intercourse.

Intimacy is anything that creates closeness and connection, which are vital to the health of our relationships. People who are counterdependent under the guise of being "strong" often struggle with a fear of intimacy, but their intellect, success, wealth, and other accomplishments or accolades can trick them into believing that they have their life all together, have a healthy state of mind, and are the strong person to rely on. Deep down inside, however, they are wrestling with their desire to be seen but are too busy hiding themselves through their acts of goodness and strength. At the root of counterdependency is a lack of trust of others, which can stem from a wounded childhood that included neglect, abandonment, a lack of emotional validation, or an insecure parental attachment during the formative years of life.

Although our childhood can have a major impact on how we grow and evolve, our adult relationships can also be deeply complex and traumatic, which may result in counterdependent behaviors, especially in our romantic lives, if we consistently experience being let down by our partners or people we thought were our true friends.

SIGNS OF COUNTERDEPENDENCY

- You refuse to seek or ask for help because you perceive it as a form of weakness.
- You cut people out of your life easily if they get too close, vulnerable, or intimate.
- You feel like people can't be trusted and you project your hurt from past relationships onto new people.
- You experience discomfort when being vulnerable and become anxious when a person gets too close.

- You can come off as egotistic, entitled, and self-centered from your inability to see the needs of others.
- You have many friends but complain of feeling lonely and lack closeness because you refuse to be vulnerable and participate in developing connection.
- You have a history of repeated failed relationships due to an inability to compromise and care for the needs of your partners, focusing primarily on your own needs instead.
- You're the strong friend who knows everyone's business, but no one knows anything about you because of your lack of vulnerability and fear of closeness.
- You're addicted to working to distract yourself from your emotional needs and to avoid intimacy.

Because American culture is very egocentric and individualistic, it's created a belief that to thrive we must be independent, and it is a personal failure not to be. This ideology can push people into a state of hyperindependence, causing them to believe that they do not need others to survive, which goes against our biological nature to need co-regulation, care, nurturing, and connection to thrive and live an abundant life. We've sold ourselves this idea that once we pass through the stage of infancy, we stop building secure attachments, and we are expected to engage in a level of autonomy that reduces the need for building healthy relationships.

It is not true that we don't need people. What is true is that we hurt ourselves and engage in a cycle of self-harm when we tell ourselves that closeness and connection are unnecessary for living a fruitful, happy, and healthy life. Being strong and avoiding intimacy are not the badge of honor you think they might be if you are left feeling depressed, unhappy, lonely, and unfilled. Avoidance simply pushes us further away from the source of growth and the joy we seek. The goal is to learn how to engage in healthy dependence by leaning into community and tapping into the resources available to us through help, advocacy, and collaboration.

OVERCOMING COUNTERDEPENDENCY AND ENGAGING IN HEALTHY DEPENDENCE LOOKS LIKE:

- Exploring unhealthy patterns that have led to failed relationships and confronting the roles you play in them
- Challenging your beliefs about what help and support looks like
- Admitting that you have flaws and not seeing them as a sign of your value or morality
- Engaging in hobbies that require trust, team building, and guided direction (e.g., volleyball, swimming classes, pottery classes, sewing, etc.)
- Challenging cognitive distortions (e.g., making assumptions about people, jumping to conclusions, taking things personally) that impact closeness by writing them down or speaking them out loud
- Exploring the root of your distrust through the lens of intergenerational trauma and rewiring the family system through new behaviors

- Exploring your definition of intimacy and assessing whether your actions are aligned with achieving it or moving yourself further from it
- Engaging in positive self-talk to combat negative beliefs or thought patterns

There are remedies all around us to help us become well, healthy, and whole. Let today be the day that you allow yourself to take off the mask, remove the superhuman costume, and give yourself permission to be soft. You can't hide yourself and expect to be seen.

Finding Remedies for Growth with Our Hands and with Our Art

There was a time in my adult life when I asked my mother if she would be willing to participate in family therapy with me to resolve some of the issues we were having related to boundary crossings and unhealthy communication patterns. I was not surprised, to say the least, when she told me no. My mother has always known I see a therapist personally, and though she never criticized me for it, I could sense from her demeanor that she was astounded, but she never projected her qualms onto me. Although I was not surprised by her answer, it still left me hurt and even upset that she was refusing to participate in something that I valued. It was something that I had to process on my own with my therapist, and the more I engaged in my own healing work, the more I became aware of something that was very distinct to the repairing of my and my mother's relationship. Going to therapy was a cultural privilege, not simply because of access, but because my mother grew up in an era when therapy was weaponized to condemn BIPOC and in a country where it was heavily stigmatized. The process of going to therapy for me seems straightforward; when you need help with managing stressors in your life or have areas you would like to improve upon, therapy can be a beneficial resource. However, for people like my mother, my grandparents, and folks from older generations who are BIPOC, the act of going to therapy could feel like putting yourself in harm's way, and that is an additional layer of repairing and healing that people from my mother's generation may need to go through that I may never understand.

In the BIPOC community, therapy and mental health are still heavily stigmatized. Overwhelming data suggests that people who are members of the Black community, specifically, may avoid seeking mental health treatment due to believing having mental health conditions means you are "crazy," and believing that issues like depression and anxiety are a form of weakness and can be managed by working harder and choosing not to give up. The strong Black woman trope can also be applied to the avoidance of treatment, since studies show many Black people believe that because we have faced many barriers and multiple forms of adversity, tapping into strength is all we need to do to combat mental illness and manage our mental health. When stigma related to mental health is addressed in BIPOC communities, it often overshadows something very critical, which is the truth about how we came to believe in these harmful narratives in the first place, and the impact of historical oppression that has roots in the health industry and has distorted the idea of mental health among those who are BIPOC. The cultural stigma surrounding mental illness exists as a product of racism, medical mistrust, and continued oppression institutionally and systemically.

My father was born in 1935, when Jim Crow laws were still in effect in the American South. Black people couldn't use the same bathroom, attend the same school, or even swim in the same pool as white people. What was also happening during this time was forced sterilization among BIPOC, immigrants, people with disabilities, and poor people. This forced sterilization was known as eugenics, the practice of human breeding as a means for "advancing" society and "reducing" human suffering. Although this practice is no longer considered ethical, victims have not received reparations of any kind, and regardless, the trauma they have endured is irreversible.

In modern-day society, medical mistrust in BIPOC communities still exists due to the disparities people of these communities face in regard to mental health and medical treatment. According to the American Psychological Association, the psychology workforce is made up of 86 percent white clinicians, 5 percent Black, 4 percent Asian, 4 percent Hispanic, and 1 percent who identify as multicultural or from other racial/ethnic groups. In the past, there was a lack of culturally competent care, and it is still lacking, which results in BIPOC reporting receiving inadequate and poor care. BIPOC are also less likely to be included in research studies related to mental health disorders, which means their experiences and symptomatology are not included in treatment considerations and may be overlooked when outlining a diagnosis. This can also lead to misdiagnosis, a common issue BIPOC face. Reducing stigma is labor that individuals in their communities are often expected to perform, and this is not just microcentered work; it is also macrocentered. Communities can thrive when the systems and institutions they need to lean on and interact with care about their well-being and are making decisions that are for the betterment of society and the of people who play a role in helping society function.

As much as I may have wanted my mother, friends, and others to participate in therapy, I also respect their boundaries and understand their reluctance, even as a therapist myself. My parents did not grow up in an era where they could easily find resources on the internet or read viral mental health content on social media and be encouraged by the masses to go to therapy. When they hear the word "therapy," they are thinking of an experience that is the opposite of what I am able to live through and experience. Although it may take a lot of unlearning for my mother and other BIPOC from older generations to reframe their perception of mental health, it's also worth understanding that not everyone is going to go to therapy. Believing that therapy is the only healing tool that exists can be detrimental to our growth.

People are not doomed if they decide to opt out of therapy as a healing practice. It does not mean that they cannot build the skills needed to manage their traumas, develop coping skills, and manage stress and adversity. This is the reason I create daily mental health content on Instagram, to promote healing work for people who may never choose to go to therapy, and for those who desire to but find it inaccessible for a variety of reasons. When we have access to resources, we can increase our opportunities to grow and evolve. Resources can be found by reading books, watching free TED talks online, listening to podcasts, enrolling in online courses, attending conferences, and being committed to learning. When it comes to mental health and wellness, a plethora of resources are available to us if we are willing to seek out what we need to heal.

One of the most valuable resources that many BIPOC have is cultural roots and practices passed down from our ancestors that have informed how we care for ourselves and our communities. We have been healing for generations through the acts of using our hands, cooking, dancing, making art, making music, bonding, and more.

My father was a very quiet man at home. He'd sit around the dining room table with his head propped up by his hands, eyes glassy and the lines across his cheeks and forehead telling stories of what was going on in his head as his record player would release tunes from Otis Redding and Sam Cooke asking someone to ease his troubling mind. Music was my father's healthy dose of escapism. He would never tell me what he was thinking, but I knew whatever it was, the music that filled the house every night was the medicine his soul truly needed. If it wasn't that, on the weekends we would have sancocho night. A few of my siblings would come over and we'd eat—they'd drink, play music, and bring out the big steel soup pot that has been through generations and fill it with potatoes, corn, yuca, chicken, pig's tail, and more. When my father was in good company, he was a different person, and in my eyes, I perceived his change in demeanor to be what looked like healing. He was not so quiet anymore; he released whatever kept his mind troubled through laughter, bonding over good food, and being in the presence of good, loving company. The safety of being around family is what allowed him to get through the sorrows of life up until his death. I may have never gotten the chance to know what caused his mind trouble, but sometimes people's burdens are not our business. Whenever I would ask what was wrong with him, he wouldn't tell me, and I know he most likely knew that what he held was not for a child to carry. It was not my place to force my father to share what he was uncomfortable or uninterested in sharing, and the same goes with my mother.

Trying to force my mother into therapy was not a reflection of community-care. I had needs that I wanted to express and be validated, but so did she, and trying to place my needs above hers by forcing her into a system she did not feel comfortable engaging in would be unfair. Instead of expecting my mother to bend and adjust for me, I found ways to honor who she was while also doing the work of managing my own struggles and learning to find ways to adjust to our relationship. I worked on myself while engaging with my therapist, and my mother worked on herself while engaging in nature. Gardening is what brought my mother restoration. Putting her hand to the soil, digging up roots, and planting seeds while out in the sun is how she released her struggles and invited in peace. She was a different person when she was outside planting, and it was clear from watching her grow her garden that this was the source from which she found her joy, healing, and strength. The simple act of helping her pick out flowers and talk about where to place them was an invitation into deeper connection and bonding that also helped us to improve how we communicate.

To be well and whole will require us to look to our roots and restore the practices that have been destroyed or devalued over time as a critical component to our healing as BIPOC. Food has always been at the center of BIPOC cultures. When we eat, we give thanks—for some it is to the universe, to others it's to God, or for the hands that not only prepared it but harvested it and allowed it to make its way to our tables. When we are eating together, we are bonding, and therefore who is at the dinner table matters. Gatherings are rooted in both safety and celebration. It means that I can exist in this communal space without having to worry about someone being a threat to my well-being. Differences can be honored, but harm cannot. Creating sacred bonds is essential for our growth, so who we bond and interact with is intrinsic to our evolution. When we are bonding over food, we may also be bonding to music that is heavily nostalgic. There's a reason why "Before I Let Go" and the Electric Slide are staple songs in the Black community. It's the nostalgia, alongside the endorphins being released in our brains, that elicits a healing space, one safe enough to allow us to let go freely in rhythm and dance.

Being liberated and embarking on the path of healing, growing, and evolving do not have to mimic the practices of the Western world and white American culture. As BIPOC, we owe it to ourselves, our ancestors, and the generations to come to be firmly rooted in our culture and uphold its values. Here are some reflection questions to help you engage in cultural healing practices:

- In what ways does food play a role in cultivating connection in your family as well as with friends? What does the concept of gathering and bonding over meals mean to you? Think of a time when you bonded over a meal. Where were you? What was significant about the conversation? Who were you with?

- What specific traditions and customs do you celebrate in your culture? What is the significance of these customs or traditions? Are they something that you see yourself passing down to your children, as well as to the children you are helping raise who are not your own? Why?

- What kind of music is specific to your culture? What impact has music from your culture had on you? What are two songs that elicit positive memories and have great meaning to your culture as a whole? What is that meaning?

- How do you honor the language spoken in your culture? Even if you do not speak your native tongue, what is your perception of your native language? How was it derived? How was it passed down or lost and why?

- What is your culture's relationship to nature? What rituals and practices have deep meaning when thinking about all sentient beings? How do you honor the earth?

- What beliefs and customs does your culture associate with death? What practices do you engage in to honor loved ones who have passed? In what ways do you celebrate the living?

- What cultural practices do you engage in that honor movement of the body or care for the body to promote healing? Is it dance?

Reiki? Yoga? How do these practices help you feel more connected to your mind, body, and spirit?

Black folk across the diaspora, Indigenous people, and people of color deserve to heal, and we owe it to ourselves to examine the ways oppressions and racism have distorted our view of our own cultures and customs and have caused us to lean into certain methods of healing that may not be beneficial or in alignment with who we are and what we believe to be true about ourselves. So much information is stored in the brain and body as well as in the mind and spirit that can allow us to deeply transform our way of being. We all have roots, and even if we feel like we have been disconnected from them, we can find our way back to ourselves through learning our history and reengaging with our customs, as well as by cultivating new ones that run through the family unit.

Healing is not a one-size-fits-all approach; there are various ways to heal and be whole. You are required to learn and figure out what healing practices are beneficial for you, your needs, and your well-being. Although there is still so much work to do on a macro level when it comes to healing the wounds inflicted from this country, we can start creating the safe spaces that we seek, instead of waiting for others to create them for us.

> Healing is not a one-size-fits-all approach.

— 4 —

THE STRUGGLE FOR UNCONDITIONAL LOVE

Healing (or Terminating) Parent-Child Relationships

When I walked into my office, I found a referral on my desk from the Administration for Children's Services (ACS) for thirty-year-old Melissa. Her three-year-old daughter had been removed from her custody due to her engaging in a public verbal altercation that led to someone calling the police for threats she had made to cause someone physical harm. As a result, Melissa was mandated to attend parenting classes as well as to see a therapist. Her case ended up in my hands, and when she arrived for her intake session, it would be the beginning of one of my hardest cases, and the breakthrough Melissa needed for her own healing.

At the backbone of society is the family unit, but the family unit cannot exist without community-care. The proverb "It takes a village to raise a child" is a reminder that community-care is an active form of child care.

Families, as well as members of a community, play a pivotal role in the socialization of children, which gives children the skills they need to contribute to society and be active members of change and progression for themselves individually, but also interpersonally and systemically. However, when a family fails to meet the basic needs, both physically and emotionally, of their children, this impacts not just the child but the family as a unit and the next generation. And because families are integral to society, communities are also at risk for being impacted by the ruptures between a child and a caregiver.

What happens at home does not stay within the walls of our home—it goes on the journey with us, it is there during the formation of our relationships, and it is a window into the different ways many of us need to reparent ourselves to be better friends, partners, colleagues, and most important, caregivers. This window is what Melissa had to peek through to understand herself better. Her history was holding her back, and if she continued down the path she was on, she would remain stuck in her trauma while her child remained stuck in the system.

The Wounded Child

During my intake session with Melissa, I completed the ACEs (Adverse Childhood Experiences) questionnaire with her, and she scored a ten out of ten. From young, Melissa was failed not just by her family but by members of her community. She was often exposed to community violence that included hearing gunshots and fights through her window, and she had an emotionally and sometimes physically violent relationship with everyone who lived in her household, including her mother. Melissa described her mother as someone who was easily frustrated, and as a result, she was spanked often in childhood for the slightest reason, and her mother's voice always raged throughout the house. Other family members like aunts and uncles were casually in and out of her home, and whenever they were there, fights would break out that sometimes Melissa was a part of. To avoid the physical and emotional abuse, Melissa wandered the streets in search for care and connection; however, this led her into the arms of abusers. At her age, she was too naive to know the difference between love and abuse because in her world, love was earned, and it was also intertwined with violence.

As Melissa grew into a teenager, her tolerance for abuse began to shrink, and instead of being the timid child her trauma caused her to be, she learned the tactics of her abusers and retaliated. The old Melissa who was yelled at, hit, and popped in the mouth for anything, and who stayed silent and submissive, was now quick with her tongue as well as her hands. Anyone who attempted to bring her harm would have to face her fists, and that included her mother. As Melissa described her childhood to me, her affect was flat; she stared off into the distance toward the wall and never made eye contact with me. It was as if a switch had been flipped, and her emotions had been completely turned off. But then I asked her a question about her daughter, and instantly it looked like the switch was turned back on when I saw the tears well up in her eyes. She never wiped them; she let them glide down her cheeks and fall into her lap. "I love her so much," she said as her voice cracked. "I want to give her a better life than my mother ever gave me."

The relationship that Melissa currently had with her mother was still centered around verbal abuse and conflict, and their relational dynamic had Melissa living in survival mode, constantly in a fight-or-flight trauma response, because trust, safety, and care were something she never experienced. This resulted in her having a low emotional IQ, where she not only struggled to self-regulate but lacked empathy and care for others. Melissa's brain perceived any form of conflict or disagreement as a threat to her safety and well-being, so she immediately felt the need to protect herself in ways that would make her oppressor small, the way she felt small when she was being abused. In response, Melissa would become enraged and lash out, become physically violent, and make threats when it felt like she was losing control or if people were getting too close and intimate.

As stated in chapter 1, growing up in a dysfunctional family has a long-lasting impact on the developing brain. Childhood trauma can impact an individual twenty to thirty years later, no matter how far removed they are from their experiences of abuse and helplessness. Family dysfunction can manifest in different ways and is not always directly linked to physical abuse.

DYSFUNCTIONAL FAMILIES CAN MANIFEST AS:

- Parents or caregivers who have addictions (drugs, alcohol, gambling, hoarding, etc.) that impact the well-being, safety, and stability of the family unit
- Children witnessing abuse (physical, verbal, emotional) between caregivers and other family members

- Children being neglected physically (lack of food, improper clothing, unstable housing, financial instability that impacts the caretaker's ability to provide the necessities for a child's development) and emotionally (emotional withdrawal, being ridiculed and called names, poor educational development)
- Parents parentifying their children: Assigning eldest children with the task of being head of household (especially after the death of a parent or separation/divorce), caring for their younger siblings, having to engage in adultlike responsibilities to care for other family members, not allowing a teenage child to be autonomous and independent (move out, move to another state for college, get a job) because they have to care for their siblings or caretaker
- Enmeshment: Parents who aim to live vicariously through their children, are overbearing, and don't respect their child's boundaries; who force their children to do the things that make them as a parent happy and not the child; and who have an authoritarian role that forces the child to be compliant and have no sense of self or not be able to form their own identity (can manifest as forcing religious beliefs, politics, and traditions onto children)

Melissa's exposure to a variety of harmful experiences left her battling complex, chronic trauma. She lived with the belief that if the people closest to you can cause you harm, then those who aren't family can cause even greater harm, which resulted in her guard always being up and her emotional barometer turned up high, ready to react and explode on anyone who she thought was standing in her way. Another layer to this, however, was that now Melissa had a child. So in the spirit of trying to protect herself, she was trying to do everything she could to protect her daughter, and it made her even more guarded, but to the point of her own detriment.

Melissa's rage did not allow her to see people as humans; she saw them as threats, and therefore, she did not care how she spoke to or interacted with others, nor did she see value in community and connection. But Melissa had to learn that there are consequences for how you treat people. People do not owe you kindness or respect when you decide you don't want to give it, and treating people as if they are the ones who caused your trauma will keep you pushed out of community instead of welcomed into it.

During my work with Melissa, she would ebb and flow between rage and vulnerability. Shortly after our first intake session, when Melissa revealed so much of herself, she immediately retreated and pushed me away. She had done something that she wasn't used to doing: she was vulnerable, and she had invited me into the sacred parts of her life. The divulging of this information fostered connection and closeness, something that scared Melissa, put her outside her comfort zone, and left her feeling out of control.

It was clear, however, that Melissa wanted help. She would call me during my off-hours or during times we were not scheduled to have sessions and leave me voice mails expressing how sad and hurt she was and that she really needed to talk to me. And then when we would get on the phone, her fight-or-flight responses would kick in, and she would instantly become irritated and annoyed and begin yelling after sharing something deeply intimate that she volunteered to disclose. This dance of rage and vulnerability was Melissa's ambivalence at play. She'd call when she knew I wouldn't answer and she could leave me a voice mail, a one-way conversation that didn't require her to reflect or go too deep because no one was on the other end of the line to engage her. But when I was there, listening, asking questions, engaging, it was not so easy for her to digest or even participate, so she'd cut our calls short or have an outburst if she felt things got too uncomfortable for her.

During stages of healing, it is normal for people to live in two conflicting states where they are seeking change but desiring homeostasis. It's like playing an internal game of tug-of-war: one side is pulling and nudging at you to stay the same and exist in your comfort zone, while the other side of you is pleading for change, new habits, and to disrupt the things that are not working and causing you harm. Ambivalence toward change can exist for multiple reasons. Changing requires you to swap the familiar for the unfamiliar, which induces fear and anxiety; the reward for change may not feel immediate or satisfying; and last, there are risks involved because change, even when it's positive, can disrupt a person's life, friendships, relationships, and all that they have known and built their life around. Melissa's goal was to be reunified with her daughter, but the process that it would take to get there would require her to face some hard truths, not just about the people in her life but about herself, her choices, and the risk of staying the same.

The Mother Wound and the Never-Ending Search for a Mother's Love

While I was working with Melissa and capturing her family history, almost all our sessions centered around the relationship she had with her mother. During one of our sessions, Melissa shared, "My mother never made me feel like she cared about me growing up. The moment she got a new boyfriend she'd disappear on the weekends and leave my siblings to take care of me; she never asked about my grades or how I was doing in school, and when she was home, all we did was fight and she'd speak to me like she didn't even like me. That's why I was running the streets from young." Melissa's face was weighed down with sadness as she spoke with a great sense of righteous anger. "Every time I call her and try to talk to her, all she says is judgmental shit about how she never got her kids taken from her, and I'm like, okay, meanwhile you were abusing and neglecting us and had me wandering the streets 'cause you didn't care. I don't care about anything she has to say; she's dead to me." The anger in her voice was firm and heavy.

"What motivates you to call her?" I asked. "It sounds like your mother is a great source of your pain, and you say that you don't care about anything she has to say, but I notice that during every session you mention that you called her again. What's motivating you to pick up the phone and choose her out of all the people you could call?"

Melissa was silent for a moment, then shrugged her shoulders. "I don't know why, actually," she said as she began wiping the tears that were beginning to well up in her eyes. At this moment, the guard Melissa was so used to having up was coming down, the walls she built around her softening.

"I can sense the conversations don't go as you have hoped when you call her, so what do you wish having a conversation with her was like? What are you hoping to hear?" I asked her.

Melissa was quiet again, and then her tears started to slowly march down her cheeks. "I love you. I'm sorry. I miss you. You can come stay with me. I'm here to help you." Melissa's voice started to crack as she spoke. "Come over for dinner. Let's spend some time together. How can I help with the court case? Honestly, anything. I wish she'd say anything else other than the things she says." Melissa was weeping now, wiping the wetness off her face and holding back her sniffles. "I don't know why I keep wasting my time, because all she ever does is piss me off every time we speak."

Melissa is not the only wounded child to consistently give their parent(s) chances, despite the harm and abuse they've caused. Feeling you've lost the love of a parent is not the same as losing the love of a friend or partner; these people are not meant to love us unconditionally, but it is the job of a parent to care, love, and nurture their children unconditionally, even their adult children. Never being able to experience this is not easy to digest or accept, and the realization that your parent may never be able to love and care for you the way you desire is dismaying. Regardless of the hurt, pain, and rejection that Melissa's mother caused her, she was still her mother, and Melissa, like everyone else in this world, is wired to seek maternal affection.

Bonding with a caregiver is a natural, biological response for an infant child. Healthy bonding helps make the child feel safe, nurtured, and protected in this new world they are born into and must learn how to navigate. However, not all children are able to experience healthy attachment with their mothers. John Bowlby was a psychoanalyst who formed the theory of attachment. He believed that attachment allowed for psychological connection between human beings and that emotional bonds between caregiver and child during the child's early stages of life had a tremendous impact on their evolution. Through his work, he delineated the four now well-known attachment styles:

- **Secure Attachment:** A child who displays secure attachment feels confident that they can depend on their caregiver. They may exhibit distressing symptoms when separated from a parent, but the return of the caregiver induces feelings of joy. Though this child might be upset to see a caregiver leave, they feel secure in knowing that the caregiver will return and not abandon them, making space for them to safely rely on the caregiver to meet their needs.

- **Ambivalent Attachment:** A child who displays ambivalent attachment does not feel secure that their caregiver will return for them. The caregiver's departure causes major distress, and the child is not easily comforted by other adult figures or even when the caregiver returns.

- **Avoidant Attachment:** A child who displays an avoidant attachment style usually does not seek comfort or attention from their caregivers and often displays no preference between a stranger and a caregiver. This is often the result of experiencing abuse and neglect, which then leads to struggles with building intimacy and connection.

- **Disorganized Attachment:** A child who displays a disorganized attachment style may present with behaviors that display both fear and joy toward the caregiver. They often seem confused, disconnected, or disoriented. This is the result of being raised by a caregiver who is inconsistent when it comes to responding to their child's needs, and it manifests as being distant and disconnected from the child physically or using fear-based tactics, like yelling, spankings, etc., to respond to the child's bids for care and attention.

Bowlby believed that attachment was necessary for survival and that infants are biologically predetermined to ensure that attachment occurs through specific behaviors such as crying, smiling, crawling, babbling, and more, which ensure proximity and contact with the mother. Though children are born helpless, they quickly become aware of behaviors that stimulate attention and care from their caregiver. This helps explain why that despite being abused, a young child will still yearn for its mother's love, because the child is programmed to understand that the mother is supposed to love them; the problem is the mother does not always know how. A mother's ability to bond with her child is essential for the child's development, and when the attachment is continually disrupted, it can lead to results in cognitive, social, and emotional difficulties for the infant in the long term. Bowlby characterized this issue as the maternal deprivation hypothesis.

SYMPTOMS OF MATERNAL DEPRIVATION INCLUDE:

- Delinquency
- Affectionless psychopathy (inability to feel remorse, empathy, affection, or concern for others)
- Depression
- Cognitive disorders

Although Melissa is no longer a helpless infant in search of her mother to supply all her needs, she is an adult child who yearns for closeness and connection through the mother-child bond. Due to Melissa's history with her family, she most likely grew up having an avoidant attachment with her mother because she experienced neglect, inconsistent parenting, a lack of structure, and varying traumas. As far as other primary caregivers, Melissa's father was also inconsistently in her life. He'd be present for a moment and then disappear and be hard to reach the next, and though aunts, uncles, and her maternal grandmother played a role in raising her, they, too, were sources of trauma for her, which stemmed from intergenerational dysfunction that didn't just start with Melissa's mother; it ran deep within the family tree. Her whole life, Melissa was surrounded by people who did not know how to love her or meet her basic emotional needs both as a child and as an adult. Underneath Melissa's destructive patterns, aggression, and combativeness, her inner child was making bids for attention and pleading to be seen and nurtured by her mother.

On Instagram, I came across a viral image a father posted of his sixteen-year-old son snuggled up in his arms sleeping on his chest. His caption said something to the effect that his son will never be too old to be held and loved by his father. In the comments section, it appeared that many people were dismayed by the image and had negative things to say about the father-son dynamic, expressing that the son was too old to be hugging his father in that way, and some even suggested the father was coddling his son too much, which would result in the son being weak and emotional. It's misguided to believe that we outgrow the desire to be nurtured by a parent, and it's misguided to believe that parenting has an expiration date. Parenting never stops; however, as the child matures through different stages of life, the parent-child dynamic will shift as the child gains more autonomy and independence. Parenting a fifteen-year-old will not look the same as parenting a five-year-old, which won't look the same as parenting a twenty-five-year-old. Adult children generally have an increased need for distance, leaving the parental home to gain a new sense of agency over their lives, explore their personal boundaries, and create new relational dynamics that may lead to family building of their own. But an adult child will never be too old to seek a parental hug.

An adult child will never be too old to seek a parental hug.

Melissa was suffering because she constantly found herself feeling like that sixteen-year-old child who wanted the love of a parent through a gentle hug, yet never got it. She also could not imagine having no contact at all with her mother. Despite what might have felt like a tug-of-war between her needs and her desires, Melissa was aware that she was not ready to create a world for herself that did not include her mother in it. So, this meant we had to find a way to help Melissa suffer less in her relationship with her mother. This would then require Melissa to lean into both grief and acceptance. She would have to learn to accept who her mother was, while grieving the person she wished her mother would be.

Parents Are People Too:
Their Stories Matter and So Do Their Children's

"I moved in with my aunt and grandmother temporarily," Melissa shared during our video session. At this point in treatment, the coronavirus pandemic had forced us into no contact and shifted all our in-person sessions to virtual.

"How is that going so far?" I asked.

"Terrible, she's—"

"Don't be talking shit about me. I'm old, but my ears still work very well," her grandmother interjected in the background, her voice echoing loudly, though she wasn't in sight.

"Would you mind your damn business," Melissa growled back angrily. And that was their dynamic every time we met for a session.

During this time, Melissa was going through something many other folks were dealing with at the height of the pandemic, being forced to stay indoors with people they lived with whom they did not like, couldn't tolerate, and had dysfunctional relationships with.

"What do you think it was like for your mother growing up now that you are living in your grandmother's home?" I asked Melissa one day in session as she vented to me about her frustrating living situation.

"I never used to think about that until I spoke to my mother over the phone recently and she heard my grandmother yelling and said, 'Now you get to see what I had to deal with when I was a kid.' Even watching how my aunt stays away from her is also very telling."

At this moment Melissa paused, and I could see she was in a state of reflection, as it was etched all over her face. "I know my mother had a rough life, but I don't really know all the details. She never talks about it, but I imagine it was hard, especially from the era she grew up in. My uncle been in jail, my other uncle was on drugs, and my aunts are just as terrible as my grandmother—they all must've turned out how they did because of her, and maybe my grandmother's mother was terrible too. It's all just a terrible cycle, one I need to break." It was the first time I had ever heard Melissa consider that her mother had a history and a story that could potentially be the road map to understanding what made her mother who she was, which would also help her see what her mother is able to give in the context of a parent-child relationship.

The Stories Our Parents Hold

Disclaimer: Before you proceed, this section does not apply to parents who were abusive, nor does it excuse abusive parenting. Abuse is deliberate and intentional and will be discussed in another section of this chapter.

We are all shaped by our upbringing, experiences, and environment, and when we get the opportunity to learn more about the intimate details and lived experiences our parents have had, we are able to humanize them and recognize that the term "parent" does not mean "perfect." When we decide to see our parents as humans who have needs, desires, struggles, and traumas, it can be a window into understanding their personal makeup. Being a parent is not a person's only identity; there is more to someone than their caretaking role, and that identity is complex and full of nuances. People never live in categories of black and white; most of the time, we exist within the gray area of life, within the ebbing and flowing of joy, confusion, happiness, grief, compassion, sorrow, and more. There is a myth that parents should be fully healed prior to having a child, and although there is some truth to that, it is not as black and white as it seems in theory, and it's also an inaccurate description of what healing is.

Healing is not a destination; it is a journey that we embark on and navigate until we depart from this earth. What is true is that people are responsible for doing the work needed to process their wounds and heal their traumas throughout their life, and this can be most important to do prior to making a choice to raise a child; however, the other side to this is understanding that adversity, trauma exposure, and situational factors that impact our well-being and mental health are also part of the growing pains of life and do not have a termination date. While parenting, the things you thought you were healed from will come back to go toe to toe with you, and healing is a dance that you will now have to navigate with a toddler at your hip trying to get your attention because kids are too immature to understand what you are going through. Not only that, but life can bring forth new troubles, and parents must take on the task of figuring out how to navigate these new hardships while operating from whatever place of emotional maturity they are in and making choices that are beneficial for them and their kids' well-being, even if their kids do not see it that way.

Parents have the additional pressure of trying to figure out how to do right by their children, on top of wanting to do right by themselves. It is a role that requires self-sacrifice most of the time, especially for women who are always confronted with having to make a choice between family and everything else we desire while facing the grueling realization that we cannot have it all.

I am two years younger than my mother was when she had me; however, at this age my sibling had already been born. If I had to put myself in my mother's shoes, but living in this current time, I would have to reflect on what it would be like to raise a child in a global pandemic, a racially oppressive world, and a society steeped in misogyny, patriarchy, poor economic structures for wealth building, poor access to health care, and high exposure to social and physical determinants of health that impact the quality of life, such as food apartheid, gentrification, climate change, and more. Sometimes we must put ourselves in our parents' shoes to understand what it means to see our parents as people first. This allows us to make space for compassion and, most important, understanding. Parents are fighting struggles that impact their well-being and sometimes their ability to be the best parent. Even when they are giving their best, parents may still inadvertently cause harm to their child. As an adult child, you must recognize this about your parents. And as a parent, you need to acknowledge that two things can be true at once—even in the midst of trying to do better, you may make choices that hurt your children.

But you can make space to listen to their pain just as you would want your kids to make space to listen to how you struggled to better understand your humanity and intentions. It can be hard to know that the choices you made as a parent may have harmed your child. This is very difficult for parents to think about because most of the time, they want what is best for their child. I observe this dynamic often and see how tempting it is for a parent to just say, "Well, I did my best," and shut down the conversation. But because parents are people, too, they must be willing to hold themselves accountable and acknowledge that in the midst of doing their best, they may have caused pain. When parents and their adult children make space to hear each other's experiences, it leads to healing and deeper intimacy within the parent-child relationship.

SOME WAYS PARENTS INADVERTENTLY CAUSE HARM TO THEIR CHILDREN:

- Not asking for help when you are a part of a community that has vocalized its willingness to support you and instead choosing to suffer in silence (this is ego work at play)
- Displacing your frustrations and anger onto your children because you are mad at yourself for your own shortcomings and struggles
- Parentifying children and assigning them adultlike roles and responsibilities to make up for an absent parent (or your own lack)
- Making your child responsible for your emotions as well as for fixing them
- Poking fun at and calling your child names, which impacts their self-esteem

- Embarrassing your child and breaking consent (e.g., sharing personal information with the family that they shared with you in private or recording their punishments to broadcast on social media)

The more Melissa dug deep to understand her mother's history, the more she also learned that her mother was still in a place in her life where she was living in survival mode. She was quick to engage in combativeness, judgment, and aggression to manage interpersonal conflicts and was not building the tools she needed to heal her own traumas. The wake-up call for Melissa, however, was that everything she saw and described in her mother, she also saw in herself, and that pained her. If Melissa wanted to break the cycle of dysfunction in her family, she would have to start with herself.

Melissa is not the five-year-old girl she was when she was first exposed to trauma; she's now an adult who is responsible for her choices, as well as her healing, and she was learning that the hard way. Melissa was always in and out of court for the same reasons. She was dealing with her trauma in ways that were not healthy for her and her daughter, and unfortunately, her daughter was paying the price for it just as much as Melissa was, from the constant removal into foster care and the disruption of the family cycle at such a young age. While Melissa worked on repairing the relationship she had with her mother, she would also need to begin repairing her relationship with her daughter and doing the work needed to close her case and ensure her last court date would officially be her last court date moving forward. "In ten, fifteen years, my daughter might look at me the way I look at my mother for causing her to go through all this, and that pains me," Melissa shared dejectedly. "I just don't know where to start." The emptiness in her voice echoed loudly.

"You start with what you have and then you go from there," I said to her. "You start with the self-awareness you have. You start with knowing what your triggers are. You start with paying attention to your needs, and you build from there, because we can't go back, but we can use what we have right now to learn how to move forward and change what isn't working."

Melissa's homework was to begin working on boundaries and radical acceptance of her mother. Consistently exposing herself to triggers without the tools needed to regulate and manage them was not working in her favor. And because Melissa struggled to accept the reality of her situation with her mother, every time she experienced painful or uncomfortable feelings, it resulted in harmful behaviors. I worked with Melissa on creating a relational plan that would teach her how to erect boundaries with herself whenever she engaged with her mother while also giving her the tools to practice radical acceptance. The relational plan below is an outline of how we approached boundary setting. Melissa first needed to learn how to identify her triggers, both emotional and somatic, and then we used this information to help Melissa identify where her self-efficacy lies. Too often, we feel powerless in the midst of conflict, but we have to remind ourselves that although we cannot control other people, we can control how we respond to people, and that is what it looks like to set a boundary with yourself.

- **I feel triggered by my mother when she:** Speaks to me rudely and is judgmental.

- **My triggers manifest as:** Me feeling threatened and having negative or violent thoughts, wanting to physically fight her, my chest getting tight, feeling enraged and heavy breathing, lashing out and cursing.

- **When I feel triggered by my mother, I have the power to:** Tell her I'm ending our conversation; tell her I don't like when she's judgmental, which makes it hard for me to talk to her; reduce the number of times I call her during the week.

- **I have the power to regulate my emotions by:** Calling a friend, calling the foster family to speak to my daughter, going outside for a walk and watching TV to distract myself.

- **It's possible my mother might not respect my boundaries; if this happens, I can remember my choices:** I can decide how often I attempt to communicate with her, I can remind her what my boundaries are, I do not have to speak to her when I feel threatened or unsafe, and I can end our calls.

- **Risks involved in having boundaries with my mother:** She might not want to talk to me, she might be upset, she might yell and scream and still be judgmental.

- **Positives of having boundaries with my mother:** I will see a decrease in my triggers, it will prevent me from lashing out when I feel like I'm being pushed to the edge, I'll gain more peace in my life by knowing what to expect and managing my expectations.

- **To have peace in my life, I might have to be willing to accept that:** My mother will not change, I will not have the close relationship I desire with my mother, my daughter may not have a close relationship with her grandmother.

- **Acceptance of this will allow me to:** Feel less angry and triggered by my mother, be less aggressive toward others after my mother gets me upset, break the cycle of me and my daughter being exposed to harmful family members.

Radical acceptance is critical for healing trauma and managing adversity. Learning distress-tolerance skills can help people manage what feels unmanageable in the moment. The hard truth is understanding that life will not always go our way. It is our responsibility to figure out what we will do for ourselves and our well-being when we are confronted with that realization. Sometimes we spend our days wrestling with the truth, trying to beat it into submission and force things to work out the way we hope. In response, our mental health suffers and so does our well-being. In parent-child relationships, it can be hard to face the reality that your parent can't be what you want them to be, but learning to accept them for who they are will give you the space to determine how you engage and interact with them and allow you to tap into your own locus of control—which makes space for healing parental wounds. Accepting reality does not mean tolerating abuse or dysfunction. Radical acceptance means learning to observe life through a solutions-focused lens by identifying the problem, observing the significance of the problem and its impact on your life, and then defining the best solution to move forward without treating the problem as if it's your identity. Instead, you see the problem as an experience and one that you can play a role in changing.

> **Radical acceptance means learning to observe life through a solutions-focused lens.**

Too often, we believe the solution is waiting for other people to change—or fighting, arguing, or exhausting ourselves to the point of no return as we wait for other people to make better choices to support the relationship, as if we are powerless. This leads only to anger and rage that can result in harm toward others and even toward ourselves. We can get stuck in victim mode by assuming our healing is dependent on other people making choices that serve us, instead of us making choices to better serve ourselves. And what we must remember in the end is that we are always going to be held responsible for our actions, no one else—not your parent, a friend, an ex, or whoever you are the angriest at. It's *you* who will have to face the consequence of your choices, whether they are good or bad.

It took months for Melissa to become comfortable with our relational plan, because healing doesn't happen overnight. With the implementation of the practices she was learning in our sessions, Melissa was beginning to express fewer feelings of frustration, I was receiving positive feedback from her caseworkers, and most important, Melissa was finally starting to have the breakthrough with her mother she had been working toward.

"I had dinner at my mother's house yesterday," Melissa said with a sense of joy in her voice. "She invited me over and I was hesitant about going at first, but I'm glad I went. We didn't argue, we cooked together, talked a little, and watched TV. I think we still have a long way to go from here, but that was a nice start." I listened as Melissa shared how the visit with her mother went, and I could sense that her inner child was finally starting to feel a sense of nurturing from her mother. Making space for grief and the realization that her mother could not be who she wanted her to be also helped Melissa make space for possibilities by exploring who her mother was and deciding what a relationship with her could look like.

Terminating Difficult Family Relationships and Knowing the Signs of Abuse

The quality of your relationships matters. To manage your well-being, you might at some point come to the realization that the relationship you have with your parents is not worth the impact it's having on your mental health. It can be hard to be an adult child to a parent who raised you but who is also the source of your triggers, stress, and frustration, instead of being a source of peace and comfort. As adults commit to the pursuit of happiness and increase their knowledge around mental health and its importance to the sustainment of our well-being, those who have parents with toxic tendencies are beginning to be more cognizant of their relationships and the behaviors they tolerate, even from family. Studies show the most common reasons adult children cut ties with their parents are past and present emotional abuse, conflicts regarding personality, political and family values, and differences regarding family roles and expectations.

Outside of my work with Melissa, I have worked with many adults who struggled with emotional abuse from their parents and made a choice to minimize contact and enforce stricter boundaries, or decided to terminate contact altogether to sustain their mental health and well-being and protect themselves from the constant emotional injuries often induced by their parents. Common complaints clients have shared were parents who were dismissive of their boundaries and who refused to honor their needs and requests for space and privacy.

VIOLATIONS OF AN ADULT CHILD'S PRIVACY CAN LOOK LIKE:

- Gossiping and sharing your child's business with family members without their consent
- Showing up to their homes unannounced after they requested you call in advance
- Keeping tabs on them or requiring to know their whereabouts (this can come off as controlling and takes away from the adult child's autonomy)

Values, beliefs, and family differences also can play a role in why adult children might decide to cut ties with their parents. When you are a child, the values your family has get placed on you without your consent. You are taught from young what your family views as good or bad and right or wrong, but when you become an adult, you can start to define your own beliefs and values, separate from your family's. However, in some cases, these differences in values can cause tension and strife, and some adult children have found it is not worth subjecting themselves to a certain level of pain and ignorance in order to maintain a relationship with their parents.

CLASHES IN FAMILY VALUES BETWEEN AN ADULT CHILD AND THEIR PARENTS CAN LOOK LIKE:

- Parents having racist views and projecting them onto their adult children (also causes conflict when the adult child is dating, married to, or has mixed-race children with someone of the race the parent is bigoted toward)
- Parents having oppressive and hateful views and ideologies toward members of the LGBTQ+ community
- Parents forcing their religious beliefs onto their grandchildren without their adult child's consent, or going against their boundaries to not raise their child in a particular religion

Abuse has a long-lasting impact on a person's well-being. When you are a child, you are basically helpless and need an adult figure to rescue you from whatever abuse you have been subjected to. However, as an adult, you will learn that you have the power to rescue yourself and make a choice to protect yourself from harm. In many cases, children who grew up with emotionally immature parents can suffer from abuse in varying ways.

SIGNS OF EMOTIONALLY IMMATURE PARENTING:

- Criticizing you when you are displaying difficult emotions (sadness, fear, shame, etc.)
- Engaging in tactics like the silent treatment, defensiveness, and blame to absolve themselves of their harmful actions
- When you were a child, responding to your crying or emotional needs with violence (spanking, ridiculing, punishments, etc.)
- Blaming you for their anger or uncomfortable emotions
- Making you responsible for fixing their feelings
- Failing to take responsibility for how they hurt you
- Withholding love and affection
- Believing love and connection can be bought through materialism

Growing up around emotionally immature adults often leads to the eradication of healthy emotional attachment and development that remains even in adulthood. Emotionally immature parenting can also lead to toxic parenting styles, abuse, and various forms of neglect.

CHILDHOOD ABUSE AND NEGLECT CAN LOOK LIKE:

- Being left unsupervised, and uncared for with the expectation that a minor can care for themselves (and their siblings, if any)
- Not being provided with food, clothing, shelter, proper tools for hygiene, a safe environment, etc., to meet a child's basic

needs. Financial insecurity is not illegal, but failure to be
financially secure enough to have children can result in a child's
suffering, instability, and exposure to harm (in some states,
denying financial assistance to help your child can be seen as a
form of neglect)

- Committing financial abuse against your child (identity theft,
  using their social security number for credit cards and loans,
  committing fraud in their name, etc.)

- Sexually assaulting or raping a child or willingly allowing the
  assault to happen, willfully ignoring a child's report of rape or
  sexual assault

- Exposing a child to sexual acts (porn, sexual conversations, or
  sexual activities in front of a child, etc.)

- Allowing your child to witness and be exposed to domestic
  violence (and also expecting your child to protect you during a
  domestic violence dispute)

- Physically harming a child (striking them with a belt, an
  object, etc.)

- Emotionally abusing a child (calling them names or talking
  down to them, withholding love and affection, guilt-tripping
  them for being autonomous)

- Intentionally injuring your child for attention, financial gain, or
  to keep them helpless and dependent on you (a mental illness
  known as Munchausen syndrome by proxy)

- Withholding proper education from your child (purposefully
  not sending them to school, denying a child access to help for
  their educational advancement)

This list does not cover every single aspect of childhood abuse and neglect, but it is a window into understanding the many ways an adult figure or parent can cause harm to a child—whether it is intentional or not. Adults who were abused as children may grow up to have complicated relationships with their caregivers, as you witnessed with Melissa. Emotionally immature parents may engage in hostile tactics to manipulate what they are seeking out of their relationship with their children. They may struggle with embracing their adult child's autonomy and desire for separation, especially when they spent their lives depending on their children to meet their emotional needs, and especially when they are dealing with loneliness and do not have a partner to emotionally depend on.

TACTICS EMOTIONALLY IMMATURE PARENTS MIGHT USE WITH THEIR ADULT CHILDREN THAT CAUSE RELATIONAL RUPTURES:

- **Guilt-Tripping:** Making statements that are accusatory, judgmental, or shaming (e.g., "You don't hang out with me anymore ever since you started dating." "You only get one mother." "What if something bad happens to me?")

- **Gaslighting:** False narratives used to induce confusion and alter a person's reality about a situation (e.g., "I never spanked you as a kid." "You're not remembering your childhood the way I do." "You're imagining things because you were angry, that's all.")

- **The Silent Treatment:** Refusing to communicate with a person or acknowledge their presence, even when you live with them.

The silent treatment can be used as a manipulative tactic to punish others, control a situation by creating a power imbalance, force someone to comply with their requests, or even get them to apologize for harm they did not cause, in order for the person to speak to them again (e.g., a parent does something that makes their adult child rightfully upset, the adult child expresses their frustration and hurt, and in response, the parent withholds communication on purpose to avoid accountability and demands an apology from their child in order to move forward)

- **Emotional Blackmail:** Using a person's emotions to weaponize a situation or pressuring you to be compliant when you resist meeting their demands (e.g., "You shouldn't have a relationship with your father. He left us, remember? You need to choose who matters more to you. I won't talk to you anymore as long as you're talking to him." In this case, emotional blackmail can be used to cause division and get you to side with them and their needs. It may also include threats: "I'll stop supporting you financially if you keep talking to your father.")

- **Disguised Hostility:** Hatred and aggressiveness being expressed under the guise of friendliness or humor (e.g., "My jokes about you not being able to invite your partner to dinner because you're gay were meant to be funny; you're being too serious.")

- **Humiliation:** Purposefully talking down to, making insensitive jokes to (or about), or speaking poorly about someone to their face or publicly to others (e.g., "If you lost weight, you probably wouldn't have a hard time dating and finding a partner.")

People are not wired to be constantly exposed to emotional violence, and at some point, those emotional injuries will have an impact on the child's well-being. For adult children, dealing with parents who lack remorse, are unable to hold themselves accountable, and are emotionally abusive can be difficult to deal with, especially when the parents do not have the desire to change.

Termination of a parent-child relationship can be a difficult choice, but sometimes it is a necessary one. During the contemplation phase, adult children may struggle with wondering whether they are making the right decision, and whether they should continue to cling to hope once more to see if things will change. What's important to remember is that a parent-child relationship is indeed a relationship, and in relationships, when pain is caused, it must be addressed head-on. You cannot control how the person who caused those wounds will react, but you can move forward knowing you were brave enough to speak up and address the things that are harmful, and you can use their response as feedback for how you should engage with them moving forward. Sometimes we want our parents to know better, but depending on their level of maturity, intellectual health, and emotional IQ, they may still have the emotional IQ they had when they were younger. Age does not equal maturity—so sticking around to see if your parents will grow wise with age is not a bet worth making.

When considering the choice to cut ties with your parents, it can come down to this simple question: Is this relationship worth what it's

Is this relationship worth what it's costing me?

costing me? And as you explore this question, it's worth assessing whether you have played an active role in trying to repair the relationship and address the issues, or a passive role in hoping your parents would be the ones to do the repairing. If it's the latter, as mentioned before, your parents may be oblivious to whatever the harm is and have no idea their behaviors are toxic and abusive. As you work on contemplating whether it's possible to stay in touch or you need to create permanent distance between you and a parent, here are some things worth assessing to give you the confidence and clarity on how to move forward.

TO REPAIR MY RELATIONSHIP WITH MY PARENTS, I HAVE:

- Made attempts at repairing the dysfunction that exists in our relationship and even exhausted my ability to continue to try
- Made attempts to be assertive and express my needs and boundaries
- Made attempts to have the hard conversations that are needed to address the wounds that were created
- Made attempts to allow them to reconcile

A healthy relationship requires the consent as well as the active participation of two people. Although a parent will always be a parent, which creates a power imbalance, adult children are still people, and in order for a relationship to work between parents and their adult children, parents have to be willing to release their grip of authority over their adult child and see themselves as imperfect people who cannot hide behind the label of parent to excuse their harmful behaviors. In some cases, an adult child might come to the realization that despite their attempts, their parents are constantly a source of great pain, and the only boundary left is to remove themselves from the relationship.

Cutting ties with your parents is a choice that requires intentional self-care and active participation in community-care. If you are considering taking this next step, here are some ways to plan and tools to use for healing as you embark on this journey or continue on a journey that may have already started a long time ago for you.

Find support from others with shared experiences: Group therapy can be a safe place where people gather in support of one another with the same common struggle and goal in mind. You can google local group therapy sessions on family estrangement in your neighborhood. If you are unable to find any, also consider seeing whether there are any online groups that engage virtually.

Find support from a professional: Therapy is also a safe space where you can not only get emotional support but also use that time more intimately to dive deeper into your emotional wounds and process your past in a more intimate way. I encourage seeing a therapist who engages specifically in family therapy and has a background in working with clients who are estranged from their parents or families.

Ask for help: This is an important time to speak up and be open with people you feel safe with in your community to garner their support. Estrangement from a parent or your family can feel lonely, so it's essential to make sure the people who care for you know how they can best support you on this journey. This is not a time to prove how strong you can be by trying to handle things on your own; instead, this is a time to seek care and comfort from those who have expressed a willingness to support you. (And when you feel like you don't have this kind of safe and intimate support, it's important to find it; group therapy, meet-ups, etc., are great places to start.)

Engage in community-care: Although we are bonded to family through blood, we are all biologically wired for connection and belonging. It's important to remember during this time that bonds can be cultivated outside of our family origins. A person does not have to share the same blood with us for us to consider them family. We have permission to redefine family in our own ways that are suitable for the life we desire to live.

Don't be compelled to let others convince you what is right for you: During this journey, you might come across people who are not supportive of your decision and will try to sway you to make a different choice, or who might even try to play mediator to get you to repair issues with your parents. It's not uncommon for siblings and other family members to attempt this. What's important during this time is to remember your why and to begin developing language to erect boundaries with others who are not supporting your decision. You get to decide how much you are willing to explain to others to help them understand your decision, but when you get to a point where you feel like you are not being heard,

You get to decide when it is time to disengage.

remember that you get to decide when it is time to disengage. People will not always understand your decisions, and it is not your job to convince them that you are wise enough to know what is right for you and your well-being.

Remember that feelings aren't facts: During this process, you will feel a range of emotions, including, at times, guilt and shame. Remember that guilt means "I did something bad," while shame means "I am bad." You might hear these voices in your head telling you that you are a bad person or that what you are doing is bad, but it's important to remember that our emotions are influenced not just by our actions but by societal norms and outside values and beliefs. When we carry feelings, we are almost always carrying someone else's opinion as well. You must do the work of reframing this irrational guilt into reality by reminders such as "I am not a bad person for not wanting to be emotionally abused by my parent."

Practice mindfulness: Often when we make big decisions in life, the process takes us away from the present and into the future, which breeds what-if scenarios. Staying present allows us to recognize that our decisions are based on what we need in this current moment, and that what we need tomorrow, next month, or in five years might be different. Right now, we are all living for today and making choices that will help shape a better tomorrow. There is no way to know what the future will bring, but practicing mindfulness every day allows us to rest in the here and now and takes away the pressure of having to live for both today and the future. Our future is dependent on where we stand in our current moment. Make the best of it by leaning into your truth and letting the days unfold without trying to force or control outcomes.

As I mentioned before, healing is a journey, not a destination. As you embark on this journey of estranging yourself from your parents or family, be open to the process of healing, which is the ebbing and flowing of grief and gratitude, loss and joy, pain and happiness. Use the exercises below to get you through this process, one day at a time.

Exercises

Create a Relational Building Plan, similar to what Melissa created earlier in this chapter. Think of a family member who you are having a hard time with relationally, and use the same framework below and answer each prompt in a journal.

- I feel triggered by my family member when they:
- My triggers manifest as:

- When I feel triggered by my family member, I have the power to:
- I have the power to regulate my emotions by:
- It's possible my family member might not respect my boundaries; if this happens, I can remember my choices:
- Risks involved in having boundaries with my family member:
- Positives of having boundaries with my family member:
- To have peace in my life, I might have to be willing to accept that:
- Acceptance of this will allow me to:

You may have decided that it's time to cut ties with your parents, caregivers, or someone else within the family. Create an emotional well-being plan by answering the prompts below:

- I will get support from:
    a. A therapist
    b. Group therapy
    c. A friend/family member
    d. All of the above

- When I feel guilt or shame for my decision, I will remind myself that:
    a. _____
    b. _____
    c. _____
    d. _____

- When I forget my why, I will remind myself that I cut ties with my family member because:

  a. _____

  b. _____

  c. _____

  d. _____

- People I am not tied to by blood but I consider family:

  a. _____

  b. _____

  c. _____

  d. _____

- I will practice mindfulness by:

  a. Journaling

  b. Meditation/breathwork

  c. Engaging my five senses

  d. _____

  e. _____

  f. _____

  g. _____

— 5 —

THE STRUGGLE FOR INTIMACY

Moving Through Loneliness
to Foster Partnership and Friendship

Dating is exhausting." I pouted to my therapist during our session one day as I shared with her another failed experience and went through my roster of prospects, which had led to nothing substantial.

There was the guy who showed up to our date with a wedding ring and told me he was married but separated, and didn't plan on getting divorced. Then there was the guy who was getting touch happy and tried to put his hands in places without my consent all because he paid for my pancakes and bacon. I can't forget about the multiple men with girl-friends or wives at home who were looking to make me their side chick. And last, there was the guy who I gave too many chances to because I had an overromanticized idea of who he was in my head, even though the version of him that existed in my thoughts never aligned with who he was in real life. I stuck around waiting, hoping that one day he'd change, he'd be the person I imagined he could be, and it would all be worth it in the end. I allowed myself to be blinded by potential because I was so hungry for love and companionship that I was willing to settle for the bare minimum, even though it left me unhappy and drained.

"I've been thinking about texting him," I told my therapist. "I know it's dumb, but I'm tired of being wise. I just want to trick myself into thinking he's changed, and this time, things will be better." My therapist stared at me, giving me the Black woman side-eye, and then we both laughed because I knew what she was going to say before she opened her mouth, and I also knew what I just said out loud wasn't getting me anywhere closer to the kind of relationship I knew I deserved. Once the chuckles subsided my therapist responded, "I have some homework for you!"

I know what it feels like to be in a place where you know better, but you don't want to do better. You just want the temporary satisfaction despite knowing the long-term consequences. You tiptoe on the edge of desire, knowing if you step in any further, you're entering dangerous territory. As a single woman who desires a long-term partnership and children within a family structure, I've been on the edge, and I've also wandered countless times into knee-deep territory that almost felt too hard to get out of due to desperation and desire. I've chased men simply because they were familiar. I've ignored red flags because I was clinging to potential and the ideas I created of a guy in my head. I've tolerated dysfunction because I didn't think I deserved any better or feared being alone. And I also know I'm not alone in this.

Many people, particularly single women, from what I notice in my own line of work, hold shame regarding their mistakes when it comes to those they chose to date or partner when that turned out not to be the best choice for them. We beat ourselves up for missing the red flags. We look in the mirror and say, "I should have known better," and we carry on with extreme feelings of guilt for participating in relationships that were not good for us. Because at the core of it all, we just wanted to be loved and nurtured and reap the benefits of companionship through a partner, something that a friend cannot give. Although it is true that sometimes we make poor decisions from a place of poor judgment, the motivation behind the behavior is often a particular reward or outcome that we are seeking, which is ultimately companionship of some kind, whether short term or long term. This does not mean we should not hold ourselves accountable for the partners that we choose, but knowing the reason why we choose people the way we do can be meaningful as we explore and delve into relationships.

In our society, people tend to think in black and white, so they will characterize a person's desire for a relationship as a lack of self-love, without considering the duality of our emotions, and that it is quite possible to love yourself and still seek to be loved by someone else. You can also have high self-esteem and still make poor choices regarding a partner or a relationship. It is perfectly normal and healthy to desire romantic partnership; after all, we are innately wired for connection and thrive when we are in healthy relationships, which play a role in co-regulation. Relationships also have the added benefits of family building, and the integration of two lives helps increase community-care and personal support. There is value in relationships, and single people have a right to want to participate in this kind of relational structure and should not be shamed for it.

The Grief of Singleness and Ambiguous Loss

For a long time, whenever I expressed my frustrations or struggles with being single, I was greeted with curt responses that often left me feeling despondent because I realized that these kinds of conversations were not safe to have among some of my peers. I've been told things like:

- "You need to work on loving yourself; that's all that matters."
- "If you aren't happy single, then you won't be happy with a partner."
- "The right person is going to appear; no need to put yourself out there."
- "You need to be fully healed from everything you've gone through before finding a partner."
- "You're young—you don't need to worry about a partner right now." (This is usually said by someone who married their high school sweetheart at age twenty-one and has never been single as an adult.)
- "Why are you still single anyway? What's wrong with you?"

Single people must navigate a special kind of grief, not only in the process of dating but in their communities when they are greeted with aloof and insensitive comments from their peers. Dating is an act of opening yourself up repeatedly while having to heal from rejection, breakups, ghosting, deceit, and more, until you find a partner that fits closely with your values and there is unequivocal interest from both parties to pursue something further. Single people must return to their beds, turning hopes and desires into faded dreams and people into ghosts after realizing this person you invested your energy in is not coming along any further on the journey. It's tiring, to say the least, and it's also significantly impacting people's mental health.

With the rise of dating apps, online dating culture has become the norm. People are using technology to make and find social connections, which is a great thing, but knowing the authenticity or intention of the users can be difficult to assess solely online. One example of this is revealed in Netflix's *The Tinder Swindler*, a documentary about a young man who was emotionally manipulating women and conning them out of their money by engaging in acts of love bombing. He'd impress them on their first dates with lavish trips and expensive items and confess his love for them early on, only to then use emotional coercion to persuade them into financially supporting his lifestyle—all in the name of love and concern that his "enemies" were out to get him. But in fact he was the villain in the story. Many of us are also aware of shows like MTV's *Catfish*, where real people made fake profiles, using a stranger's picture, to develop emotional connections with others just for the other person to find out they were being manipulated and lied to, also known as being "catfished."

Developing trust in online spaces is possible, but it can be difficult, and although these are extreme examples, many people are experiencing situations that don't even make it to TV. I think about the guy who showed up to our first date with his wedding band on and proceeded to gaslight me and make me seem as if I were crazy for having an issue with it—when he had told me online that he was single. Studies show that people who frequently use dating apps report higher levels of anxiety, depression, and stress. Users report dealing with high levels of rejection and disappointment. Self-esteem and body image are also impacted when you are chronically ghosted or fail to receive matches or interest from other users. In order to combat the negative impact online dating can have, make it a positive experience by having boundaries and most important, be up front and communicate your intentions to make the experience more satisfying and less anxiety inducing for the users involved.

Ultimately, dating and singleness are rooted in a particular kind of grief, known as ambiguous loss, that is hard to pinpoint because there truly are no words for it, and it often goes unacknowledged. It's easy to grieve with someone and offer your condolences when the loss is tangible. We do it all the time when a loved one passes away or when a particular tragedy occurs: People will send flowers, we mourn and hold funerals, and there's a plethora of Hallmark cards that express sentiments of care and support. But when the loss cannot be felt or even seen, it can become hard to grasp as real to some; therefore, it's usually ignored or even dismissed. For single people, it can be hard to deal not only with the grief that comes from being single, but the other layer of grief at play when the people around you lack the empathy and the intellectual range to see the sadness that can come from being single and to acknowledge it with sensitivity and kindness, rather than labeling these sad emotions as a lack of self-love and sharing rebuttals on how much one needs to heal or love themselves to gain a partner.

We are never fully healed as people because healing is not a destination, nor is there a finish line waiting to be approached as we navigate certain seasons in life. Healing is a journey and a process, and what people need to know is that healing happens in relationships. We learn about ourselves, our patterns, our needs, and even our dislikes when we are relationally bonded to others. The very first relationship we encounter that teaches us about ourselves is the relationship we develop with our parents. We are taught many things about who we are, and even what we think we can or can't be, from the foundation that is laid through the parent-child relationship.

However, bonding does not stop there. We grow and mature and begin to find safety in other relational dynamics when we go to school and explore the world away from our parents. We develop friendships and learn new ways to bond with others outside our family of origin. Even if we grew up in unhealthy, dysfunctional families, we can find others who are safe for our nervous system, and learn what it means to co-regulate when we are surrounded by people who are healthy for both our mind and body. I say all of this to emphasize that it is simply not true that in order to date and find a partner, you must be fully healed. In fact, it is *in our relationships* (including friendships) that we gain the tools needed to do the healing work and be better people to others and ourselves.

What's worth remembering about healing is that it requires both self-care and community-care. Too often, people believe that they can heal in isolation, and then find themselves struggling when it is time to integrate back into a day-to-day life that involves interacting with people and cultivating connections. Many people want to be seen but refuse to show themselves, and often want from others what they aren't even willing to

> # Healthy relationship dynamics are developed, not magically formed.

give. Healthy relationship dynamics are developed, not magically formed. We can believe that we are the best thing to ever happen to someone, only to find out we were their biggest headache. We can believe that we are not worthy of being with someone, only to end up finding out that they see more value in us than we see in ourselves.

When I was in a relationship with one of my exes, I still remember the day he confronted me and told me that he felt unsupported by me when I would make certain remarks to him that made him feel hurt and upset. In my eyes, I was trying to be supportive; in his eyes, I was chastising him and belittling him. We had a very eye-opening conversation where I realized he was right. I revisited the things I would say to him and owned the fact that my words often landed as judgmental, and though that was not the intention, the impact mattered. I spoke to him in ways that I knew I probably wouldn't have wanted him to speak to me, and since that day, that conversation has helped me to be more mindful in all my relational dynamics, not just my romantic ones. Most important, it allowed me to look even deeper into myself and explore why I was so quick to speak down, rather than up, and it was the result of my own past experiences and being spoken down to in ways that I did not like. It then became my native language, and I was doing unto others what I did not like to be done to me.

Relationships can show us more about ourselves than we ever thought we knew. The good ones, and even the ones that are unhealthy, can be a window into how we view ourselves and the condition of our self-esteem. If we see ourselves as people who are fully healed, we will not be able to learn and become interdependent, which is a necessity for building healthy and sustainable relationships. When we are interdependent, we acknowledge that two people are bringing their full selves into a relationship, and for it to thrive we need to compromise and value the needs of each other, rather than placing our own needs on a pedestal. Dating is the ultimate act of interdependent care, and the act of dating teaches us who is meant for us and who is not, and simultaneously helps us to be mindful of our habits, ideologies, and behaviors that impact the flow of healthy interdependent connection.

> Dating is the ultimate act of interdependent care.

When thinking of relationships and dating, here are seven things to evaluate and work on:

1. The Checklist and Overromanticizing

The concept of ambiguous loss applies to dating for a particular reason, and that is because single people often have an idea, or even a checklist, of who their ideal partner would be and the qualities they would possess. This is when a person becomes psychologically present (an imaginary person who feels real), but they are physically absent (this person does not really exist), and when single people date, most of the time they are looking for the ideal person who will match the psychological profile that they created in their mind. Two problems can arise from this.

First, we have an idealized version of a partner, and when we meet someone who matches the qualities of the person we've created in our mind, we run the risk of overromanticizing them. Before they attempt to show us who they are—meaning their character and personality—we have already found ourselves in love, married, with children, and on a honeymoon in our mind when we haven't even gone on a first date yet. This behavior can be self-destructive. Overromanticizing a person enhances our feelings for them based not on the effort they put in in real life but on the effort they are putting in in our mind. You begin liking this person so much that when they start presenting red flags, they're inconsistent, or they simply aren't treating you the way you want to be treated, delusional optimism kicks in. This is when you disregard factual information being presented directly to you because the story you are creating in your mind is much more powerful, palatable, and rewarding than reality.

Here's an example: Imagine meeting someone who matches all the qualities you are looking for in a partner, and then you find out they are not interested in ever having children. The shock of this discovery is a threat to the image and story you have created in your mind about them, so instead of believing them and taking them at their word, you continue to date them because you are optimistic that they will change their mind. At this stage, the issue is that as you hope for them to change, you begin to engage in certain behaviors to come off as more enticing and appealing, potentially thinking, "If I do X, maybe it will get them to change their mind." This is self-sabotage, and guess who gets hurt in the end? Both parties, not just you. You get hurt because reality has finally trumped denial, and you are left to reckon with the fact that your partner was telling the truth about not wanting children. And on the other end, your partner is hurt by the realization that you never fully accepted them. They have been led to believe that you accepted them for who they are and their decision not to have children, when in fact you've been working overtime to figure out how to change their mind.

Believe people when they show you who they are and listen to them when they are vocal about their truth and desires. It takes mental work and practice to stop overromanticizing, but it can be done. Begin this work by learning to practice mindfulness and detaching yourself from the outcome. We overromanticize people because we have a desire that we are trying to ful-

> **Believe people when they show you who they are.**

fill, but when it comes to dating, you may meet numerous people who are great people but not great partners. Allow yourself to enjoy the experience without getting attached to a fantasy. As you date, I encourage you to reflect on this question: "I know how I feel about this person, but how does this person make me feel?" Because you can like someone who mistreats you. You can like someone who makes you feel less than. You can like someone who causes you stress rather than brings you peace. Last, sometimes you must be intentional about changing your thoughts when they arise. If you catch yourself dreaming about your wedding day or the arrival of the kid who doesn't even exist, swap the thought by grounding yourself back in reality: touch an object, savor a piece of candy, or listen intently to the sounds around you.

Second, the other issue with the idealized version of a partner is that it generates a "type," meaning a particular kind of person that we are drawn to. A question I always get from singles is "Why do I attract X kind of person?" And we can replace "X" with "emotionally unavailable" or "not relationship ready." There is a lot to unpack here about the concept of who and what we attract. The first thing to understand is that we attract all kinds of people, not just one type. The issue is that we will overlook most of the people who are attracted or interested in us, if we don't find them attractive or are not interested in them in return. We all have standards and desires, as well as a lens through which we define attractiveness, so if you do not like a person, you will not be interested in their advances. You have a type you are seeking, and your type is ultimately what you are trying to attract. Now, when you notice that you are chronically in relationships with partners who exhibit the same kind of behavior, you must do the inner work of assessing what qualifiers you are using to determine whether this person makes a healthy partner.

Many of us have a standardized checklist of what we think makes a good-fitting partner, but too often, our checklist does not reflect the proper guidelines that would give us insight into what will create a healthy, meaningful relationship. In our society, it is common for people to view the potential of a partner by first assessing these areas: good looks, body size/shape, social status, wealth/income or job status, and educational background. There is nothing wrong with desiring any of these things in a partner or having certain standards around them, but we can put ourselves at risk for engaging in unhealthy relational dynamics if we believe that a nice face, attractive body, and good job are synonymous with being emotionally mature and available, having integrity, and

> Ask yourself, "What am I allowing, tolerating, and making space for?"

having the skills to create and sustain a healthy relationship. When you keep attracting a type of person, you must do some inner reflecting to ask yourself, "What am I allowing, tolerating, and making space for?" These people exist in your life because you made room for them to be there. And by making room for them, you push away other people who are interested in you and may desire a thoughtful connection—you just don't like them. When you like someone, that means they fit your preferences— it can be hard to reimagine a new set of standards or preferences—but if you keep making the same choices and choosing the same type of person, you will remain unhappy.

Take some time to review your checklist and how you define what makes a good partner. Opening yourself up to dating different types of people requires curiosity. You may have convinced yourself that the ideal partner is the one who matches the person in your head, but by doing so, you are not allowing people to show you who they are and who they can be to you. Dating allows us to learn about the lives of others, while also inviting them into our own lives. When you acknowledge that there is not just one type of person for you, you invite in options and can explore with this person the foundational things needed to cultivate healthy partnerships, such as values, respect, shared goals, and interests.

2. The Fixer-Uppers

People who are codependent in their relationships may have a habit of desiring partners who they presume need to be saved or fixed. This behavioral pattern can come from being parentified as a child and having to care for emotionally removed parents as well as siblings, and being praised and valued for what you do for others. It is normal to offer help and support in healthy relationships, but in codependent relationships, rescuing shows up under the guise of help when you:

- Take responsibility for other people's actions and feelings
- Put the needs of others over your own needs and suffer as a consequence
- Problem-solve for others instead of allowing them to find their own solutions
- Cater to other people's needs in order to be liked and accepted

These habits can lead to stress, burnout, and resentment. When your efforts go unnoticed or unappreciated, you might lash out at a partner or even feel inadequate because you've been taught that your value is in what you do for others, even when others are not asking for your help. You may also feel resentment that is misdirected rage. You tell yourself you are angry at others for not acknowledging your hard work, when really you are angry at yourself for going above and beyond and being self-sacrificial, unprompted.

Breaking this cycle starts with healthy boundaries. You must know where to draw the line and be mindful of your intentions when you are doing for others. Ask yourself:

- "What am I hoping to gain if I do this for someone?"
- "In what ways might this action harm me in the long run?"
- "Did this person ask for my help, or am I assuming they need it?"

3. Ignoring Red Flags

In every relationship we form, we have red flags, yellow flags, and green flags, which help us determine how to proceed in the process of building and sustaining the relationship. Red flags are essentially dealbreakers. They are signs and indicators that we pay attention to that help us determine whether this person is good or safe for our mental health and can participate in cultivating a healthy relationship. Red flags look like: people who are controlling, lying, manipulative, violent, aggressive, and so on. Then there are yellow flags. Imagine the caution sign you see when there's a wet floor. You can still proceed to walk on it, but you need to watch your step and tread lightly. Yellow flags are not blatant like red flags, but they are signs that we need to investigate through asking questions, communicating, and paying attention to patterns and behaviors that don't make us a feel good. A great example of this can be meeting someone who's a bad communicator. They take hours to respond to your texts and barely initiate phone calls, but they are big on spending time together in-person and are persistent in pursuing you. Having a discussion on what communicating looks like when you're not together can be helpful for the relationship, and a yellow flag that can turn into a green one. Green flags are signs that make us feel safe enough to proceed and build connections. Green flags look like: reciprocity, mutual interest and respect, shared values and beliefs, compatibility, authentic connection, and so on.

Knowing and discerning what your red flags and green flags are is important for forming healthy relationships, but not everyone is able to identify what a red flag is. Red flags tell us when to stop, and green flags tell us when to go, and if you grew up around very unhealthy relational dynamics, you may normalize toxic behaviors and assume you're standing in front of a green light, not a red one. You may also choose to ignore red flags because reality is a hard pill to swallow when you have a dream or idea of who someone is. Going back to point one regarding overroman-ticizing and delusional optimism, we can ignore red flags when we believe the person in front of us is not acting in alignment with the fictional person in our head. In our heads they have potential, so we may excuse certain behaviors to give them a chance to become the person that they are in our mind. Another reason many people ignore red flags is because of their relational trauma history. If you were raised by emotionally im-mature parents, having affection withheld or a lack of emotional safety might be normal for you. When experiencing emotional neglect, you may also struggle with the belief that you are the problem in all your relation-ships and do the work of changing or molding yourself to be different and accepted by your partner out of fear of losing them or their love. This inner turmoil might have you believing you need to change, when really, your partner is the problem and is most likely unhealthy for you.

To understand what your red flags are, it can be helpful to start with unpacking what the green flags are for you in a relationship. Think about your own relational dynamics both past and present.

- What characteristics does a person need to possess to make you feel seen, heard, and emotionally safe in a relationship?
- What does respect look like to you in a relationship?
- What are things that you know for sure you cannot tolerate when it comes to a relationship?
- What are the things that help you feel loved and cared for in a relationship?

4. Poor Communication Skills

Poor communication damages relationships. The first way many people struggle with communication is by not being assertive. Instead, they are passive or aggressive with their communication. It will always be our job to advocate for ourselves in our relationships to get our needs met, and when our partners come to us with their needs, it is

Poor communication damages relationships.

also important that we do the work of actively listening to assess whether we can even give them what they are asking of us. Being assertive means communicating in a clear and direct manner that honors the humanity of the other person. It means being respectful, listening actively, and responding in ways that are not belittling or degrading. It is solution focused and works to attack the problem, not the person. We can learn to be more assertive by minimizing language or behaviors that cause confusion. If you are communicating through text, for example, stop including laughing emojis to soften the message. Texting can be difficult enough to process, so when you are speaking in a serious manner, stop diluting the tone and message with smiley faces. And if you're not joking and want your point to be made clearly and firmly, stop adding "lol" unless there is something to be laughed at.

Communication also requires comprehension. Are you actually listening and understanding what you heard, or are you looking for loopholes so that you can start defending, deflecting, and projecting?

Another approach to building assertiveness is learning to be emotionally regulated to avoid reacting rather than responding. Sometimes when we are upset or annoyed, we may react in ways that are harmful to others and even the relationship, but when we take time to regulate by pausing to reflect and then respond, we learn to minimize the risk of either being passive and people-pleasing or being aggressive and hurtful.

Curiosity also enhances communication. Some people struggle with small talk, while others hate going too deep too fast. When meeting people, we are always learning about them, which helps connection and emotional intimacy. Some people also struggle with conversations depending on the format—some hate texting and would prefer a phone call, while others enjoy both but prefer face-to-face. Either way, it takes curiosity and exploration to learn about a stranger. Ensure that you are always communicating with intention, and speak up when you feel as if the communication has room for improvement.

5. Poor Boundaries

When dating, it can be important to know what your boundaries are and to communicate them. Think of past relationships and ask yourself, "What makes me feel safe physically and emotionally when dating?" A dating boundary can look like: "I do not do house dates as a first-time date. I prefer to meet at a public location." Or "I don't feel comfortable talking about this particular topic yet. I'm open to revisiting it if things progress, but for now I would prefer if we changed the subject." Know what your needs are and advocate for yourself up front.

6. A Lack of Effort

Relationships thrive when there is reciprocity. When one person is giving more than the other, they will become burned out quickly and will eventually lose interest. Putting in effort looks like: being curious about the other person, taking action to invest in the health of the relationship, and being assertive in the process of pursuing someone. When you fail to show up, are inconsistent, and make things about you without being willing to compromise, this will impact the health of your relationships.

7. Not Trusting Your Gut

The most important thing you can do when dating is trusting your gut and intuition. Don't confuse trusting your gut with feelings of anxiety. When you trust your gut, you are guided by peace and comfort regarding what you are feeling and thinking, and there is no confusion, fear, or worry. You have a sense of contentment and you're led to make whatever decisions you know needs to be made for your betterment. Anxiety, however, is rooted in fear and worry and does not lead to peace; it leads to confusion, stress, and dread. You know yourself and what you need better than me or anyone else, so lean into that self-trust and inner wisdom and apply it to your life.

Lonely, Together: When Couples Struggle to Make It Work

There is no perfect relationship, although society and the trending social media hashtag #RelationshipGoals might make it seem that way. By now, if you read the entirety of this chapter, you've learned that relationships thrive when they are rooted in interdependence. We must bridge self-care, our inner healing work, to community-care, our relational healing work. Although no relationship is perfect, healthy relationships exist and they can thrive in conflict because of that foundation. Earlier, I shared with you dating red flags and the importance of defining what yours are. Knowing the things that are full stops for you helps protect you from potential harm. Green flags are healthy signs for a relationship and yellow flags are indicators that you should be cautious but leave room to explore further. But what happens when people are already coupled? Although I discussed red flags in the context of dating, red, green, and yellow flags will manifest throughout a relationship and will continue to reveal the health of that relationship and areas where improvement can be made.

In relationships, people grow more into who they always were. It is very rare that a person's character will change into something they haven't already shown you, but often, when we ignore red flags and don't address the yellow ones, we run the risk of ending up in troubled relationships that feel more like a burden than a safe place. Healthy relationships are formed when people take the time to address the issues that are manifesting in their relationship instead of ignoring them, minimizing them, or pretending they don't exist.

HEALTHY RELATIONSHIPS ARE BUILT AND SUSTAINED WHEN:

- You and your partner practice communicating your needs
- Your expectations of each other are clear and honored

- You attack problems and not each other
- You are open and willing to compromise with each other
- You disagree in a respectable manner
- You trust and respect each other, including when there are differences
- You can grow both as individuals and as a couple
- You are interdependent, not enmeshed or codependent
- You both feel safe with each other and neither party is abusive
- You can honor each other's physical and intimate needs
- You are thoughtful and put in effort to keep the relationship going

When couples struggle to make it work, they are experiencing issues that feel like threats to the relationship. When not addressed, these threats put a strain on the relationship and may weaken the bonds that have been formed. During the 2020 coronavirus pandemic, many couples found themselves struggling to keep their relationship afloat. The divorce rate increased 21 percent and continues to rise postpandemic. The lockdown, which resulted in couples working from home and having to social distance away from friends and family, may have been the catalyst for the rise in breakups and divorce for couples who had previously been able to manage their problems through avoidance, social outings, and having separate routines that allowed them to skate over their ruptures rather than address them.

What also became a strain for couples, but particularly for working women, was the division of child care and household duties, with women being stuck with a disproportionate share. Many women reported that even though their partners were working from home alongside them, caretaking and household responsibilities still ended up falling on them, which exacerbated the stress and other mental health issues that many people were already struggling with. As lockdown continued, many working people were impacted financially, and even when we aren't in a pandemic, financial stress is one of the leading causes for divorce. Conflict over money can erupt when one partner is expected to carry the financial load, when there are differences in values around money, and when one partner exerts power and control over the finances in a way that equates to financial abuse.

What many couples had to face head-on during the pandemic was the health of their relationship and their level of satisfaction with their partners. It takes time, effort, and energy to make a relationship work, and there must be an investment from both partners. Sometimes couples will need additional care and support to help make their relationship work, which is why participation in couples therapy also increased during the pandemic. One of the best things couples can do for the health of their relationship is to acknowledge the habits and patterns that run on a constant loop and gain the tools and skills they need to create new relational patterns and dynamics to enhance the relationship, rather than drain it and their partners as individuals. Often, when we are flooded with stress, we develop habits both individually and relationally that can make our relationships suffer. However, not all habits are good habits, and it can be worth exploring the common ways we burn out our partners.

COMMON UNHEALTHY RELATIONSHIP HABITS ARE:

1. Poor Communication

A common reason why many couples struggle in their relationships is lack of communication. Often, a person in the relationship is struggling with their own cognitive distortions, which manifest as making assumptions/jumping to conclusions, overgeneralizing, mental filtering, and more, and the problem with these thinking errors is that they get in the way of cultivating healthy conversations. If you want to make your relationship work, you must be willing to speak up and address issues that arise and also share your needs. A relationship cannot thrive when there is poor communication. Healthy communication looks like: cultivating psychological safety where your partner has the space to share their thoughts, feelings, and emotions without being belittled, chastised, or shamed for expressing themselves. It also requires active listening and ensuring we are hearing our partner's words carefully—not what we want to hear in the moment to spin the situation or to make their words fit into our own projections and insecurities. Healthy communication takes work, but it will be one of the best things that you can do for your relationships.

2. Poor Boundaries

All relationships require boundaries. No matter how much we love a person, we all have needs and limits, and learning to express them to our partners is how we invite safety and intimacy into our relationships. When we have boundaries, we are not only advocating for our needs but are also taking responsibility for our actions, and we are asking our partners to be responsible for themselves and own their behaviors. Some ways poor boundaries in a relationship manifest are:

All relationships require boundaries.

- **Poor sexual boundaries:** Pretending to be sexually satisfied by your partner instead of speaking up and expressing your likes and dislikes and finding ways to try something different so that you both experience pleasure.

- **Stonewalling:** Giving your partner the silent treatment instead of engaging in communication to tackle the issue at hand. In a case where you become emotionally flooded, it's important to express this to your partner and decide what it looks like to take a break to self-regulate, and then re-engage in the conversation. However, leaving the conversation with no intention of resolving issues and becoming passive-aggressive are unhealthy.

- **Testing:** Testing your partner to see what choices they will make to help you decide how to navigate a situation is a sign of poor assertiveness and poor conflict-resolution skills. A relationship is not a game to be played, and people are not pawns. Speak up and say what needs to be said and address what needs to be addressed.

PRACTICE SETTING HEALTHY BOUNDARIES BY
REFLECTING AND ASKING YOURSELF:

- In the following boundary dimensions—physical, emotional, time, and sexual—what are three needs I have that I haven't addressed?

- In what ways am I advocating for my needs to be met in my relationship after I have communicated them? (e.g., repeating my needs, engaging in action, etc.)

3. Following the Fifty-Fifty Myth

No relationship will ever be fifty-fifty. There are going to be times when the work of sustaining a relationship manifests differently for each partner depending on the roles and dynamics at play. During season five of *This Is Us*, Kate's husband, Toby, took a new job in San Francisco, which required him to travel and be away from home a few times a week. It was clear that this left Kate frustrated, and when Toby would come home and try to be an active father, she would chastise him and remind him of the load she was carrying as a full-time mother. Kate made it seem as if Toby was taking vacations a few times a week, but she had agreed to his accepting this job offer so that it would help sustain their livelihood as a family. They were both parents to the same children, but their roles as parents and the work behind it were not distributed equally. Realistically, in any relationship, things will not always be equal because each partner will be committed to ensuring the needs of the relationship are met and deciding what their role will be to sustain that. In some cases, a new mother may decide it is best to be a stay-at-home mom while her partner works because the partner brings in most of the income, and this can manifest vice versa where a father chooses to stay at home while his partner works. This can also look like one partner taking on more household duties while the other works late-night hours. Your relationships are not a fight for equality. Things will not always be equal; instead, fairness

> **Your relationships are not a fight for equality.**

and equity are the support beams a relationship will stand on. We must learn to examine what our relationships need to thrive, and that may mean sacrifice in some areas of life to make things work. However, this form of self-sacrifice does not mean neglect of self or suffering; it simply means being flexible and compromising to respect the needs of the relationship. This level of investment must be done by both partners, not just one. The fifty-fifty myth does more harm than good. Be willing to reflect and ask yourself, "What does our relationship need to thrive right now, and what role can each of us play to ensure our relationship is getting what it needs?"

4. Not Adjusting Expectations

It is normal and healthy to have expectations in a relationship. However, there are going to be times when your partner cannot give you what you need, and you will have to compromise and find a way to adjust your expectation so that it is beneficial for you both. An example of this is consistently getting upset with your partner for not giving you good advice when you are struggling emotionally with a particular problem. It is healthy to want your partner to be an emotionally safe sounding board, but adjusting your expectations may look like accepting that your partner lacks the skills and insight to be an emotional compass for you regarding certain issues. It's not that they don't love you or care for you; they are simply unequipped in certain areas of life. You can manage this by expanding your supportive circle to have certain needs met elsewhere, such as in therapy or a friend group.

It can be frustrating to be in a relationship with someone who may not be able to meet your expectations, but it's worth remembering that staying in a relationship is a choice, not a requirement. When you run up against issues with having your needs met, doing the same thing and hoping for different results will not help the relational dynamic. Sometimes it takes adjusting our expectations of our partners to have our needs met when we choose to stay with them.

5. Complaining Instead of Repairing

When we face problems, it's natural to complain, but sometimes we can fall into a habit of choosing to complain instead of choosing to take action to find solutions to our problems. In relationships, some couples end up beating the same dead horse, which leads to stress and misery. Finding solutions and repairing issues requires you to communicate about the issue and acknowledge the impact it is having on your emotional health. Think and ask yourself, "Since I know what is going wrong, what are things that would make me feel like this is going right?" And use that to cultivate solutions together.

Building and sustaining a healthy relationship requires intention from both parties. A healthy relationship cannot be sustained on the back of one person, which is why in some cases relationships end, and people make the choice to move on. Who you decide to partner with is a big decision that can impact the quality of your life, your mental health, and your well-being. When you choose a partner, you are envisioning a particular life you believe can manifest with this individual. We choose people for a variety of reasons, and down the line, we may realize that a relationship that was once beautiful is now too broken to be repaired and that the only way to make things work is to step away from suffering and choose a life apart from each other.

We are human, and the reality is that people are learning that the work that it takes to make forever last simply isn't worth it when you are in an unfulfilling, unhealthy, unsafe, and unhappy relationship and staying would be an act of self-harm. Regardless of what the people you know think and what society thinks, you have a right to decide what is best for you when it comes to decoupling and your relationships.

Antidotes for Loneliness:
Honoring Friendships as Sacred Relationships

No one wants to feel alone, but there is a difference between experiencing aloneness and feeling lonely. Being alone can be an act of solitude. It can be sacred time spent with oneself to become more self-attuned and self-aware. When we practice self-attunement, we are deepening the connection we have with our mind, body, and spirit. It's like doing a check-in with one's energy and heart to seek clarity and alignment. In this space, you get the opportunity to observe and examine the parts of you that may feel energetically blocked or emotionally depleted. Finding stillness in a busy world can be difficult at times, and with an abundance of responsibilities that require our immediate attention, sometimes we can find ourselves gliding through life, letting the days slip into the next, without any sense of awareness regarding what our needs are and whether our actions are in alignment with our purpose, values, and the version of our higher selves that we are trying to morph into. Stillness activates us; it shows us the cracks and crevices of life that we continuously overlook because we are so busy doing and never stop to notice the parts of life that need patching, all the shattered pieces of our lives that need to be put back together, and the fractures in our mind, body, and spirit that are seeking wholeness.

There are going to be times when aloneness is a prerequisite for building healthy romantic relationships. As I stated earlier, healing work is found in both self-care and community-care, and sometimes the self-care we may need before trying to form new bonds after trauma, hurt, and heartache is a deep sense of self-attunement to guide us into self-awareness, so that we can be mindful of the habits, patterns, and behaviors we exhibit in our relationships that need deep healing work. Without self-attunement, we repeat old patterns in new relationships. We find ourselves going after the same "type." We find ourselves having the same arguments and having to rebandage old wounds that keep getting opened. In order to grow, heal, and evolve, we must be willing to give ourselves an opportunity to learn from within.

Without self-attunement, we repeat old patterns in new relationships.

When you are hungry, you are in tune with your body and know that it needs to be satiated. When you are tired, you are in tune with your body and know that it needs rest. But what happens when you are emotionally wounded? Are you in tune with yourself both physically and emotionally to know when you are experiencing emotional dysregulation? Are you aware of how your body responds to a person when they are not good for your nervous system? Do you understand why you experience migraines, muscle aches, chest tightness, or even stomachaches around certain people even when you are in good health? Have you ever taken the time to assess whether this is less about a medical condition and more about being emotionally triggered or activated, and whether your body may need care, rest, and attention in that moment?

The more you are aligned with yourself, the better you can take care of your nervous system. This does not mean that you need to run off to a silent retreat and spend twelve days in the woods with your thoughts, feelings, and emotions to practice solitude. You can practice aloneness where you are.

One of my favorite ways to be still and release myself from the constant demand of busyness is taking myself out to dinner. It allows me to be more in tune with my emotional hunger as well as my physical hunger. I get to people watch and take others in, but I also get to spend time with myself and know my needs through the act of satiating my mind and body. When that's not an option, I will get in my car and just drive around my neighborhood to step out of my home and into a new environment where I can sit with myself, my thoughts, and feelings as I cruise and sometimes listen to music. In my own experience as a single woman, solitude and aloneness have also helped heal the deep emotional wounds that come from rejection and heartache. The reality is that a partner is not someone I can go to a store and order at the self-checkout line. A romantic relationship requires the consent of another individual, so we have to be willing to ask ourselves, "When I don't get the thing that I seek, what will I do about it?" It means learning to tolerate aloneness while engaging in the beautiful act of connection that comes from platonic relationships.

Being disconnected from others impacts our ability to co-regulate, which is why the loneliness epidemic is hurting so many. When the 2020 coronavirus pandemic hit, social isolation became the norm for many people. Work-from-home orders kept people secluded from community and family, and that seclusion did not lighten up for many as the years have gone by. Touch deprivation also became a struggle for those who lived alone and were single, and the lack of human contact and human touch caused an increase of stress, depression, and anxiety. Human contact is vital for our well-being. US surgeon general Vivek Murthy, MD, classified loneliness as an epidemic not to be taken lightly. Being touch deprived can literally impact the body and release a hormone called cortisol, which is the culprit for issues such as high blood pressure, muscle tension, and increased heart rate, and it even impacts the immune system. Loneliness, however, is such a complex issue, because there can also be times when you are surrounded by people you love and know on a personal level, and still feel a great sense of loneliness and detachment.

SIGNS YOU ARE EXPERIENCING LONELINESS:

- You feel a great sense of abandonment from the people you care about and feel close to
- You feel a great sense of rejection and emotional disconnection from others
- You feel uncared for by people in your social circle and family
- You often feel left out or like a third wheel in your social groups

There may be times when situational factors induce feelings of loneliness, such as the death of a parent, long-term partner or best friend, moving to a new state and not knowing anyone, starting a new job, and even other life transitions like getting married, having children, starting a business, getting promoted to a more demanding role, and other dynamics that might require a shift in your ability to show up the way you used to (or had the capacity to). The answer to loneliness is not a one-size-fits-all practice or like a Band-Aid to cover a wound that really needs stitches. Sometimes you have to go back to a place of self-attunement to assess the root of loneliness and to do the work of exploring the different ways you may be hindering yourself from forming deep connections as well as the ways you may be struggling with vulnerability and allowing yourself to be seen in order to cultivate healthy connections.

Studies show that close friendships and face-to-face interactions can help combat loneliness. Friendship is such a sacred relationship, and when we form healthy friendships, we are ultimately improving the quality of our lives. I've known one of my best friends, Nequa, since we were six years old. We met in first grade and have managed to maintain our friendship for over twenty-five years. Nequa and I are very different in many ways, but despite our differences, at the root of our friendship is trust, respect, and most important, reciprocity. Over the course of these twenty-five-plus years, we've hit some bumps along the way, but we have been able to maintain our connection through open communication, a willingness to compromise, and doing the work of having hard conversations whenever we found ourselves in a place where either one of us hurt each other or caused offense.

For most of my young life, Nequa had been my only best friend, so when I left high school and found myself restarting my friend group, since most of my other friends and I went in different directions, I was closed off to the idea that it was possible to form another close and deeply sacred relationship. I had been living with the assumption that a best friend is someone you knew since childhood, and if you didn't meet them then, you'd be missing out on this kind of relationship altogether. Well, luckily I proved myself wrong when I met Shantia, who happened to be my on-the-job trainer. Shantia is six years older than me, and as soon as I met her, I felt cared for by someone who was like a big sister. Now, over ten years later, she remains one of my best friends and confidantes. A few years after we met, she moved out of NYC, and though it sounds cliché, the distance brought us much closer, since it required more prioritization and a willingness to make space for each other regardless of the distance between us. This meant more intentionality, which many people lack when it comes to sustaining bonds and connections.

One of the most valuable things I learned in life that has helped me form healthy friendships is that friendship falls on a spectrum. Everyone you meet or like is not your friend. There are levels to friendships that range from acquaintance to soulmate. Friendships form and evolve when there is a mutual interest in each other ther and there is reciprocity, trust, support, and a deep desire for connection. Friendships, like any other relationship, are formed through vulnerability and often compatibility. However, just because you know a little bit about a person doesn't mean they are your friend, or even your close friend. Knowing this can help with managing expectations and having healthy boundaries. For example, I would not advise asking someone that you recently met and had one lunch date with if they could loan you fifty dollars or if they would want to be your child's godparent. It does not matter how well you get along or how much you like them; they are still a stranger, you do not form a friendship after just one encounter, and you do not build trust after one encounter, either. At times we can overstep and create high expectations for people to show up for us without putting in the work needed to form a safe, trusting, and respectful relationship.

There is no clear sign to indicate when a person goes from stranger to acquaintance and from acquaintance to close friend, but we can pay close attention to subtle signs to know when we are deepening our relationships and what category a person may fall into after we form a connection with them. Friendships, regardless of closeness, are important and valuable, and it can be very beneficial to have a wide range of different kinds of friendships that fit the different needs you have in life.

The Five Types of Friends

The Situational Friend

The people who fall into this category might be coworkers, neighbors, people you talk to at the gym, at parenting groups, and so on. These are people you see frequently in a particular setting, and your connection tends to be tethered to that setting. This person may not know all your business, and they may not be the person you ask to brunch, but they are someone you look forward to seeing when you know you are going to be in a particular environment. It feels good to know that in this place, you'll have someone to talk to and bond with, even if it is just in the moment.

The Acquaintance

Situational friends can easily turn into acquaintances. This is someone who you might have small talk with, who is familiar by sight, or who might be known casually through another friend. Often, acquaintances can have casual conversations and experiences, but they may have reservations when it comes to being deeply vulnerable and sharing intimate information about oneself. At this stage in friendship, people are still in a courting phase. They are getting to know each other's character, personality, and values to assess whether closeness is even possible.

The Social Friend

Because people are so deeply complex, we might find ourselves in relationships with people we truly love and get along with but who have different interests from us. This is where the social friend comes in. It's normal to have certain friends in your life with whom your bonds are formed through a shared activity or hobby. When it comes to music, I have a versatile palate and love a range of artists. Some of my favorite artists are people most of my close friends would never want to hear in concert, and because I truly enjoy live performances, I know that if I want to go see Damien Rice or Lake

Street Dive in concert, I would call a particular friend to accompany me, and a different friend might want to go with me to see Jhené Aiko or Doja Cat. Social friends offer us the beautiful opportunity to create attachments through experiences. And while it may be as deep as the friendship goes, there is care and support, and for this person that you are able to do things in life with, which is a deeply sacred way to break bread with another person.

The Close Friend

As your relationships with others deepen, you might notice a sense of closeness start to take shape. A close friend is someone you trust with personal and intimate details about your life. You can depend on them, and there is a great sense of reciprocity in the relationship from both people putting in the work and effort to maintain the relationship.

The Best Friend/Soulmate

Some people are caught off guard by the idea of a best friend being like a soulmate, and that is because our society tends to glamorize romantic relationships over platonic ones. A soulmate has nothing to do with whether the relationship is romantic. It has everything to do with the depth of connection two people have. When a best friend is a soulmate, there is a powerful, deep connection that fosters closeness to the point where this person can feel like the family you've been missing despite not sharing blood. A best friendship is just as deep as a close friendship, but the difference might be that a best friend has more of a sacred position in your life and will ultimately have certain responsibilities a close friend wouldn't have. For example, a best friend might become the godparent of your children, but a close friend would not. Or they may hold the title of maid of honor or best man in a wedding. Having this level of connection with someone is an honor, and as with any level of friendship, it is maintained through effort, intentionality, healthy communication, and care.

What makes building friendships so hard to navigate is that there isn't clear language that if offered helps us understand the nature of the relationship. In romantic relationships, there is language to support the structure of the relationship that allows you to see where the line in the sand is drawn. There are terms like casual dating, monogamy, engagement, marriage, and polyamory. Romantic relationships even have laws in place to prepare for endings, and supportive structures to help sustain them when it seems as if the foundation is falling apart. But what do you do when a friendship feels like it's falling apart? Who do you turn to? How do you get the clarity and guidance you need to make it work the way a couple would?

Most of the time when I am working with my clients, friends don't go to therapy together. There's usually one person in the room speaking for the dynamic of the relationship. Due to the lack of language to define friendships as well as supports in place to keep them up, friendship break-ups can be hard because people don't often communicate the end of a friendship; either they begin pulling back with no explanation, or they completely disappear with no communication at all. Many people struggle with communicating their needs to their friends because we have always been told that our friends are not our partners and they don't owe us anything. It is true that our friends are not our partners, but they are valuable members of our lives and even family, and in any relationship, we will have needs and we must learn to express them.

NEEDS IN A FRIENDSHIP CAN LOOK LIKE:

- Wanting more quality time together
- Wanting less quality time together
- Wanting advice that is not rooted in judgment
- Wanting support or help
- Wanting a space to be heard and to vent in a healthy way

Yes, You Do Need Friends

Some people have convinced themselves that they do not need friends because they have been wounded by friends in the past by not having their needs met and have endured relationship ruptures that were difficult to repair or heal from. We are wired for connection. It does not matter whether you consider yourself an introvert, you still need people; you just have a different emotional barometer for closeness and may need frequent breaks from socializing compared with someone who is more extroverted. To avoid pain and heartbreak, we find ways to pretend that we don't have needs when we are used to our needs not being met. If you come from an unstable and dysfunctional family as well, it's possible you may feel that people act too unpredictably, and avoiding closeness has become your survival tactic. Many people have learned to seek comfort, connection, and support only in the context of a romantic relationship, which causes them to rely heavily on their partners and ultimately leads to relationship burnout.

We are wired for connection.

Not even our partners can be everything to us, which is why having a healthy range of social connections is a vital part of life, but unfortunately, this valuable connection known as friendship tends to be a struggle for many to sustain, and to also come to terms with when one ends. Like any other relationship, friendship breakups can happen naturally. People grow apart, and sometimes their interests and compatibility no longer align. It's important to normalize friendships ending in healthy ways.

Friendship breakups are not always the result of toxicity in the relationship. When I was in college, I had a great group of girlfriends who I did life with, and after we graduated, our lives began to take shape: some of the women moved out of state, others began having families, and all continued to live their lives. Our close, connected circle started to open and disconnect, and we all naturally went in different directions but have remained cordial throughout all these years. Our friendship did not end because of malice or ruptures; it ended because it never had the intention of being more than it was. It had served its purpose. That circle of connection got me through college, and the rest of the women through their seasons in life, and we accepted our ending for what it was. We gave ourselves the closure we needed, which was owning and understanding

> **Any connection is one worth learning from.**

that even in friendships, forever is a myth, and longevity does not have more value than short-term experiences. Any connection is one worth learning from.

Hard Truth:
Sometimes You're the Problematic Friend, but You Can Learn to Do Better

In some cases, however, friendships, like any other relationship, may end due to mistreatment, toxicity, and poor relational dynamics. A healthy friendship thrives when there is respect, reciprocity, and trust—those are the legs of the relationship that allow it to walk and go the distance. There will be times where we may meet people who do not display these characteristics, or over time things may shift in our friendships, resulting in a relationship that feels one-sided or where there's no support, care, or celebration of success and achievements. It can be easy to see the problem in others, but you must be willing to look within and admit when you are the problem and your problematic behaviors are the reason you are often excluded and feel lonely, even in friendship. Insecure attachment as a child and poor social-emotional development can impact a person's ability to gain useful skills needed to create and sustain healthy relational dynamics. In chapter 1, I talked about my experience with being bullied in school, but adults can be bullies too. A person may engage in bullying for many reasons, but two common reasons are insecurity and enjoying power and control. I've witnessed many adults exhibit bullying and mean behaviors toward their friends because of feeling envious or inadequate. Sometimes this form of bullying can manifest as something called disguised hostility, which is a form of passive-aggressiveness. Disguised hostility is when a person exhibits hostile behaviors under the guise of kindness.

EXAMPLES OF DISGUISED HOSTILITY LOOK LIKE:

- "Wow, you look so beautiful. I'm surprised that dress actually fits you after gaining weight."
- "Congratulations on your engagement. I didn't think it would happen, but I'm so happy for you."
- "I love your home; I would've chosen different furniture, but it's really nice, though."
- "Congratulations on your promotion. I'm really surprised they promoted you out of all people, but I'm so happy for you."

It's normal to feel emotions like jealousy in a friendship, but how you handle your jealousy matters. Being passive-aggressive, rude, and envious will not make people interested in offering you empathy or being their friend. This will make people close themselves off from you and choose to not share important matters because they anticipate how you will respond. Another way we can rupture our friendships is when we make everything about us and have little regard for the people we claim to care about. Sometimes we don't realize when we are monopolizing a conversation and steering the topic away from the person and toward us. If a friend calls you to vent or complain about their partner, and then all of a sudden you start talking about yourself and *your* partner, you are putting your friend in a position of having to cater to your emotions, when they are the ones who reached out to get support. Active listening is critical for the health of any relationship. If you struggle with ADHD and find it hard not to redirect the conversation, try mindful listening, where you focus and hold on to key words that you hear your friend expressing to help you stay grounded in the conversation. You might even focus on something that engages your five senses to help keep you present and not get distracted, which may potentially cause you to steer the conversation.

Returning to the discussion of loneliness, we might consider if we are lonely in friendships because we are the ones inadvertently secluding ourselves, and not the other way around. A lack of effort and inconsistency create imbalanced relationships. For example, if you are the type of friend to always cancel plans last minute *and* with no explanation, then at some point you will stop getting invited regardless of the reason. You must remember that despite what you are going through, whether you are triggered or whether you are tired, your actions land on another human being who has feelings, needs, and emotions. I am a strong advocate for boundaries, but I am also a strong advocate for applying nuance to every situation and remembering that there are people in your life who you do owe respect to instead of entitlement.

People pay attention to patterns, and if you have a pattern of being inconsistent, you are impacting someone who has a right to set boundaries with you. You might conflate this as being mean or as a lack of understanding, but you must know that people are not wired to consistently be exposed to emotional blows. This does not mean that people will choose not to be your friend, but they may choose to have boundaries in place to safeguard themselves from the emotional blows they may be tired of enduring. Learn to communicate to others what is happening with you. You might need to inform your friend that because of a chronic illness, sometimes you experience situations that interfere with your ability to do certain things; therefore you cancel. Because of your depression, you struggle with time management and get overwhelmed going places, so you may need to schedule dates late in the evening to give you more time to get ready. Because of social anxiety, you commit to things, but then fear and worry come over you, so you cancel (please note that this is still an internal issue, and until it's healed, your peers may set boundaries due to your chronic canceling). The key here is to communicate so that people can know what to expect and how to adjust. Don't treat people with little regard if you are trying to build a healthy relationship with them. Communicate and give them the information they need to understand your circumstances better and be willing to put in the work and effort to identify alternative ways of creating and committing to plans with one another.

Unlearning old patterns requires trying new behaviors. It *is* possible to develop the skills needed to become a better friend. It takes practice, self-awareness, and a willingness to put in effort. As you do the work, start by learning to improve the following.

BUILDING HEALTHY FRIENDSHIPS WILL REQUIRE YOU TO:

- **Communicate and address what hurts:** We are people with feelings, and when we interact with other humans, we *will* experience emotions in response to someone's behaviors. People may not know what is hurting you until you speak up and say something about it. Talk to your friends—they are people, too, and preserving your friendships will require you to have hard conversations.

- **Have healthy boundaries:** Even friendships require boundaries. Sometimes lines get crossed when we don't consider the level of closeness we have with certain friends, but being mindful of our place in people's lives can be important because the boundaries you have with your best friend might look different from the boundaries you have with the acquaintances in your life. Remember that just because you have access to a person does not mean you have an all-access pass to their lives, and vice versa. You are not obligated to share information with someone regardless of your level of closeness, especially when you feel you aren't close at all.

- **Compromise and be flexible:** Remember that as we grow, our needs may change, and so will our lifestyles. Your best friend who was once child-free may not have the energetic capacity to take a phone call to hear you vent after giving birth. And your friend who is child-free will not always have the energetic capacity to be available because they, too, get tired and have needs. Compromise and flexibility in a friendship look like constantly finding ways to support the needs of one another by managing our expectations and having a willingness to meet people where they are in life. As we grow and our lives change, our capacity to show up the way we used to might look different, and it's important that we honor that.

- **Have healthy disagreements:** Too often, one of the most common issues I see in friendships is believing we can control our friends and getting upset when they do not take our advice, or when we take their honest feedback as a personal attack and mislabel their difference of opinion as jealousy or judgment because we don't want to hear the truth or a varying perspective. If you are looking for a friend that you can control, you are not ready for friendship. If you are looking for someone who will agree with everything you say, never challenge you, and is a people pleaser, then you are not looking for a friend.

Just because a friend has a different perspective than you or does not agree with you does not mean that they are unsupportive. Two things can be true at once: a friend can love and care for you, while being vocal about their opinion once you've invited them into your business. A relationship thrives when there is compassionate honesty, not people-pleasing. A supportive friend is someone who sees value in you and respects you enough to be honest with you without judgment. They are not your enemy or a hater; they are truly a friend.

At the root of community-care is friendship. Surround yourself with people who lift you up, care for you, and are emotionally mature enough to accept your boundaries and communicate in a healthy manner. Connection is not a fad. The need for love and closeness will never be a phase that we go through, but a necessity for survival. Studies show that people are healthier, happier, and even live longer when they are connected to community and have a support system. Never underestimate what friendship can do for your mental health.

Exercise

- **Reflect:** Is there a friendship you currently need to advocate for that you feel is falling apart? Fill in the blanks below.

  Dear_____,

  One of the things I admire most about our friendship is _____. I feel supported by you when _____, and lately, I've been feeling _____ in our friendship as a result of you _____, and I wanted to know if you are willing to talk about this. I would love to talk this over, and if you agree, please let me know if you prefer that I call, text, or we talk in person.

- **Reflect:** What qualities and values do you look for in a friendship? What are your needs in your friendships? What makes you feel safe in your friendships? Now examine your current friendships. Do you feel like they are in alignment with your needs and values?

- **Reflect:** Consider whether you are in an expired friendship. Think about the friendships in your life. Are there any where you feel uninterested in the person, attempt to avoid them, feel annoyed in their presence, have no desire to support them, feel obligated to stay in touch, or are concerned things will be awkward if the friendship ends because of other close connections (enmeshed family, shared friend group, etc.)? Ask yourself these three things:

  1. How does staying in this expired friendship impact my mental health?

  2. How does staying in this expired friendship push me closer to my relational values and goals?

  3. What is the possibility that things can change and this relationship can be preserved? What needs changing?

— 6 —

THE STRUGGLE FOR FULFILLMENT

Easing into Rest and Finding Passion and Purpose Outside of Our Labor

A s a mental health educator and corporate wellness coach, I spend a lot of time leading keynote talks and workshops to organizations on tackling burnout and building better mental health practices to sustain personal well-being. In these talks, I often give people the space to reflect on their personality traits and identify the ways we may be contributing to the toxic system of busyness, because our self-worth is tied so deeply to productivity that sometimes we aren't even aware of the ways we keep the cycle of burnout going in our daily lives. American culture has led us to believe that burnout is a badge of honor, and the "pull yourself up by your bootstraps" message has us so disconnected from true community-care that we don't realize how hyperindependent culture is literally killing us. This is especially true in communities of color, where we face systems that are so harmful that, in some cases, we skip care altogether, both interpersonally and institutionally, and face the consequences in the form of a shortened life span, poor health, and a lack of connectedness and community. Though the term "burnout" was coined to give language to the workplace stress experienced by those working in toxic organizations, further reflection can highlight that burnout is America's way of evaluating tenacity, drive, passion, and worthiness. America has fostered the biggest toxic work environment dating back to slavery, and at this point, the inability of Black people and other communities of color to rest is another lingering symptom of intergenerational trauma. Labels like "lazy" and "unskilled" are quickly placed on Black people and people of color for resisting America's culture of urgency, busyness, and constant performance of labor for low wages in return.

The exhaustion of having to keep up and do for many manifests differently on a cultural level, but on a societal level, we are all victims of capitalism, which makes us prone to searching for what is next because labor is not as fulfilling as the American dream has told us it would be. In 2021, because of the coronavirus pandemic, according to a study done by the US Chamber of Commerce, America faced what is being called the Great Resignation, where forty-seven million people quit their jobs in search of better work-life balance, safer work conditions, and most important, increased compensation. Service workers receiving low wages made up a larger percent of folks who quit in search of higher pay and better work environments. The option to quit and advance into a new role wasn't easy on everyone, however, according to research done by Politico,

Black and Hispanic workers had a much harder time trying to advance out of low-wage jobs, due to structural inequalities and discriminatory hiring practices. In 2019, the CROWN Act was enacted to ensure protection against discrimination from race-based hairstyles such as locs, braids, twists, Afros, and more in the workplace and school systems. Data from the CROWN Act indicates that Black women are 1.5 times more likely to be sent home from work because of their hairstyle. There have been countless reports from Black parents that their children are being forced to cut their locs off to either attend school or play sports. It can be extremely hard to advance in a society with systems that are designed to be barriers instead of providing a clear path.

I often think of the dreams my parents must've dreamed from their homeland as the whispers of America the Great traveled across seas and invoked images, emotions, and sensations in their mind and spirit. A dream so immersive it compelled my father to run up against waves, stormy nights, and shallow seas as he traveled by boat to give this country his labor as a butcher, a low-wage, low-skilled job that in return helped to bring food to families who would have never considered doing the laborious work needed to get them the meals they elegantly enjoyed. I think of the sacrifices of my mother, a woman on a quest to reimagine home so much that she'd leave all she'd ever known to set out for a land she had never stepped foot on. A place where she'd end up being a housekeeper and performing domestic work to aid those who either didn't want to do the work of maintaining their homes themselves or needed assistance due to age, disability, and so on. Once again, low-wage, low-skilled work, but valuable to our society and the progression of community. As a young child, I had the pleasure of accompanying my mother to the homes she worked at—which in retrospect I imagine was quite advantageous to my mother because she did not have to worry about child care.

Watching my mother work modeled to me what it looked like to build not only self-sufficiency but also social capital. The families my mother worked for were more than just her bosses; they were networks of people who cared about her enough to help her leverage economic gain by inviting her children into their home and providing us with gifts during the holidays, meals, snacks, and even a bed to take a nap in when our little bodies were tired. My mother's kids were not an inconvenience to her employers. My sister and I being welcomed into the homes of these families made the burdens my mother had to carry a little lighter, and the barriers to building any sense of financial freedom much less of a challenge.

As I got older, I thought about how my parents had an open-door policy for my friends to come over after school, and when it was time for dinner, we broke bread with whoever was in our home. There was never going to be a moment when there wasn't enough—we would find a way to make it enough to serve those we built community with, both old and young. If I was ever locked out of my home, I knew my neighbor held a spare key. When I had to call the ambulance to assist my mother after a fall, my phone was flooded with text messages and phone calls from my neighbors, who were worried by the presence of an ambulance in front of my home. When my father died, I had other father figures in my life to help me through my grief. These experiences tell me that the American dream must be more than just financial gain. It must be more than just securing homeownership and education. It must be more than just work and labor. What good is this dream if we are imagining it without the power of community-care and connectedness?

The Power of Connectedness

The American dream stands on the premise of individualism, when in fact, community is how we advance both individually and as a society. In terms of our well-being and fulfillment as people, social capital has as much value as financial capital. There is no person on this earth who has ever built financial freedom without the help of another—the help of a friend, partner, family, a privileged bloodline, a customer, a peer, a loyal fan, teacher, role model, or network. The dream of acquiring more cannot be achieved when we are disconnected from the nurturing that comes from being surrounded by people who are celebrating you, helping you, protecting you, investing in you, and simply sharing life with you. You might think that you don't need people, but I encourage you to think about the parts of you that have been wounded by others and how creating a barrier to connection is how you've taught yourself to cope and protect yourself from future harm. Needing people does not mean having full reliance on others; it simply means sharing experiences with others so that our stories are not buried within us, but instead can be used as road maps to help build the world as we bond over experiences, commonality, struggle, and triumph. It is in *the ways we connect with one another* that change happens, both personally and in our communities, allowing us all to get ahead instead of always feeling left behind and disconnected.

Dreaming of Accountability

Togetherness is hard sometimes, because no one wants to be in a community with someone who is violent, oppressive, disrespectful, entitled, and unwilling to learn and unlearn. We may hear these words and immediately think of someone we know or have encountered, but I also encourage you to explore deeply whether you have ever been that person. The person who refused to hear the needs of others. The person who demands but never gives. The person who expects but never compromises. The person who's too entitled to respect other people's boundaries but is quick to erect their own. The person who harbors stereotypes toward others because they don't live according to your values. The person who speaks down to people to build themselves up. The person who judges and throws stones from a glass house that most likely has cracks in the foundation. Who are you when no one is watching? How do you treat people who have different beliefs from yours? How do you disagree without disparaging someone? Why do you think people should want to be in a relationship with you based on how you treat them? These are things we all must think about because *we all have the potential to cause harm—* and when harm enters the gates of our communities, we are fracturing

Who are you when no one is watching?

the bones and limbs of society. We cannot excel when we are being oppressed, and we cannot expect progression and lead an advanced society when we are doing the oppressing.

When you treat people poorly, you must assess where this level of audaciousness, as well as the entitlement, comes from. I am aware that people with personality disorders such as being narcissistic display these traits, but there are also people who live life as if the world owes them something simply based on their gender, race, and even religion, and it has nothing to do with a mental health disorder.

Sometimes your behavior is the result of depression, and sometimes your behavior is a choice that stems from the ideologies and beliefs that you uphold and choose to engage in daily. Too many of us want to cling to the "good person" narrative, without acknowledging that we are simply people who have the capacity to do both good and bad in the world. It will be our own responsibility to learn and take action to change our ways of thinking and our behaviors. You are going to mess up. You are going to fail. You are going to get things wrong, but there is a difference between mistakes and patterns.

You may be familiar with the famous quote "Insanity is doing the same thing over and over and expecting different results." Sometimes we want everything and everyone around us to change, while doing absolutely nothing to contribute to the change. This mindset can be rooted in a form of distorted thinking known as casting blame, believing everything that goes wrong is everyone else's fault and you have no contribution or control over certain matters in your life. What you will always be able to control is how you want to show up in this world, for yourself and for others. *Only you can do your accountability work*—and when you feel disconnected from community, you must be willing to look inward to examine the roles you play in that disconnection.

Accountability is not a dirty word.

Accountability is not a dirty word, though many may treat it like it is. When others expect you to hold yourself accountable, they are offering you grace, a lifeline, an invitation back into community, but with some adjustments. It's important to remember that no one is born evil or wicked, but as we grow up in this world, we are socialized in many ways, and our experiences will impact how we see ourselves and others as well as how we behave and treat ourselves and others. There are going to be times when we hurt people, and when this happens, we must be willing to be empathetic enough to look inward and ask ourselves, "What belief was I upholding when I engaged in that behavior?" and "How will I make amends and repair the ruptures that I've caused?" If I invite you into my home and you accidently break a glass, I will respect you more for owning your mistake and apologizing versus pretending it didn't happen or blatantly not caring about breaking the glass because it doesn't belong to you. It's the same with our relationships. When we build bonds and connections with people, we are being invited into their sacred space, a spiritual home that exists within their heart, mind, and soul. To be granted such an opportunity to be connected and entrusted in the space of another person is a valuable gift not to be taken for granted, so be mindful of how you care for others. We all go through things, but that does not make it okay to treat people with no regard or as if they have no humanity because you're having a bad day, feel triggered, or don't have the same beliefs. Accountability is essential for togetherness—but that is your work to do, so get started on it.

HOLDING YOURSELF ACCOUNTABLE LOOKS LIKE:

- **Acknowledging how your behaviors negatively impact others:** You are not always going to get things right. In life you will make mistakes, and when that mistake impacts, harms, or inconveniences another person, taking accountability looks like acknowledging how your decisions or behaviors landed. You may not be able to rewind and fix what happened, but taking ownership for what *did* happen can make a huge difference and create trust in communities when you show others you can be self-reflective, aware, and put your ego to the side to make space for other people's feelings. Learn to apologize for your actions up front without making it other people's responsibility to absolve you. A helpful tip when it comes to apologizing is that if you are starting your apology off like these two examples, then you are not being accountable; you are placing blame:
  - "I'm sorry that you feel that way . . ."
  - "I'm sorry, but it's your fault that I . . ."

A real apology is when you can reflect on your actions, identify the impact, and make a commitment to change moving forward. When we start our apologies off with blame, either we are saying that our actions are the other person's responsibility to fix, or we are insinuating that they are the problem for feeling how they feel instead of addressing and owning that it is our actions that induced those feelings. It's not always easy to admit when you are in the wrong, but it is through that admission that we build healthy bonds and connection.

An apology reframe: "I am sorry for _____. After further reflecting, I see how my behavior was harmful and I've learned _____. Moving forward I will commit to _____ in order to do my best to no longer perpetuate the harm that I've caused."

- **Changed behavior:** What joy is there to find in life if we do not grow, evolve, or change? If you are not growing and evolving, you are not just impacting your well-being, you are most likely disrupting your ability to engage in community because you are not taking the time to learn, unlearn, and find ways to evolve your thinking, which will inevitably shape your character, how you treat people, and the decisions that you make for your own betterment. I have worked with and even been in community with people who have caused themselves suffering because of something as simple as refusing to change their mind and taste the freedom of having a new perspective. I have also seen people, because of their bond to their history, make excuses such as "I was raised this way" or "This is what I was taught growing up," instead of making a choice to do something different. Accountability requires change, and change is a choice available to all of us. Sometimes change looks like adopting a new mindset and being open to hearing people's stories, sometimes it looks like reflecting and forming a new habit, and sometimes it looks like realizing you are living by rules you can break so that you can stop what might be self-sabotaging and causing others harm.

As individuals, we must play a role in collective healing by doing the work needed to heal ourselves so that we are not oppressing others and upholding detrimental systems and structures of power that cause harm—and this work takes a whole lot out of you. It's work that causes you to go toe to toe with yourself at times, to assess the ways you harbor internalized oppression, internalized misogyny, and internalized racism, because our beloved America is a web of oppressive forces that we all get tangled in, even when we try to resist, and it takes work to push through and advocate for social justice. I aspire to live as the highest version of myself daily because I know it is within that space that I can nurture the relationships I'm a part of through reflection, self-care, and compassion. Burnout culture will not die out if toxic structures remain in place by people in power with toxic beliefs. The more prevalent it is, the more we need to heal, both in solitude and collectively. When I am my best self, I can offer my best to others.

In a world that is always heavy with its endless traumatic experiences, we must choose ourselves daily or else this world will pick us apart. Many of us go through a great amount of unfairness, and sometimes as a Black woman, I still feel like I'm fighting to be seen as more than one-fourth human. But when I remind myself that my healing is greater than me, that it is for my future self and for my community, it helps me lean into rest and reimagine a dream where my humanity is cared for in this

American society. My self-care work is liberation work that is fueled by rest, play, education, connection, and passion. I do not want to live a life of suffering, despite knowing that suffering exists. I want to live a life where I can acknowledge the injustices of this world and never reduce myself because of experiencing injustices in this world. Trauma tells us to make ourselves small so that others can have more space, but we need to be okay with taking up space and showing up as our full selves because it is our full selves that need care, compassion, and nurture, not just the bits and pieces of us that appear well put together. In the midst of doing the hard labor to dismantle oppression, we must be willing to invest in ourselves and remember that we have a right to care for ourselves without having to earn it. We have a right to give ourselves the things we need to make what can feel like a difficult life meaningful.

> We have a right to care for ourselves without having to earn it.

Dreaming of Rest, Passion, and Play

In 2020, when the coronavirus pandemic flipped our world upside down, Disney released a movie called *Soul*, which ended up having a significant emotional impact on many adults who watched the film. In particular, the main character, Joe, resonated with many. In the movie, Joe, a high school jazz teacher, experiences dread and unfulfillment in his life because he has not become the successful musician he had hoped to be. One night, however, he gets a phone call that has the potential to change his life and catapult his career as a jazz musician. The call is from a former student of his, inviting him to play live for a very well-known singer named Dorothea. Joe immediately says yes and embarks on the opportunity. The night of the event he wows the crowd, including Dorothea, and she invites him back to perform what would be his dream gig—the thing he had been chasing that would in some way give his life meaning and purpose. Joe is so excited and absentminded on his walk home that, he falls right into a hole, straight to his death. His soul then departs his body, and in an alternate universe where all souls aggregate after death, he meets another soul named 22. Together they go on a journey to rediscover life and the little things we encounter day-to-day that fill our lives with passion and purpose, helping Joe to see that it's these little things that help give our lives meaning.

I think about this movie often, and the concept of valuing life. What it means and how to embody it. In one of my favorite books, *A Field Guide to Getting Lost*, author Rebecca Solnit writes, "Leave the door open for the unknown, the door into the dark. That's where the most important things come from, where you yourself came from, and where you will go." This door into the unknown has stood before me many times in life. The feeling of fear, worry, and trepidation on the doormat, blocking me from entering. There was a time when a character like Joe would have resonated with me. I wrestled with finding my own meaning and purpose in life separate from society's one-dimensional definition of success, which almost always equates to wealth building and is never about connection, community, and pure happiness. For too long, my eyes stayed fixed on what was known, what could be seen, felt, touched, and imagined, and I never made any space for the unknown or discomfort. My impatience never allowed me to sit through anything that wasn't ripe enough. Whatever I sought had to be both palatable and tolerable. The world already produces so much pain, and as a result, all I ever wanted was to indulge in a little bit of ease and softness. So doors that would have led me toward the unknown, into the dark, were doors I walked past.

It would take time, and feelings of regret, wonder, and curiosity, for me to realize that sometimes in life the things we want are behind the things we label with a Caution sign due to our fear, anxiousness, and fixed belief systems that have the power to take away our ability to imagine something different from what we are used to because we have taught ourselves that our way is the right way, and there are no alternatives. We must be willing to push our own boundaries, because sometimes the limits that we put in place to protect ourselves are self-sabotaging. They keep us small and unseen. Pursuing joy and happiness will always require us to extend ourselves into unknown territory, and in this space, we may find ourselves grieving our former life to make space for a new version of ourselves.

In 2020, after ten years of working as a therapist seeing clients, I decided to step away from one-on-one work and into clinical consulting, and I started my own mental health consulting agency. I knew it was time for me to step into that unknown territory. I had been desperately trying to avoid it, but I knew my happiness depended on it. When my last day of work approached, I couldn't shake the feeling of anxiety about becoming an entrepreneur and leaving traditional work behind. I was caught up in worrying about the opinions people would have of me if I told them I left a solid job and salary to start a business that could potentially backfire on me financially and emotionally.

I also had to admit to myself that a large part of my anxiety stemmed from my deeply ingrained belief that my employment status was synonymous with my worth and value, and I did not know my place in the world without a traditional job. I promised myself time for rest, play, and relaxation after quitting, and instead I immediately filled my calendar with to-do lists, conducting outreach and obtaining new corporate clients. I was working harder as an entrepreneur than I had when I worked a full-time job. For the first time in my adult life, I had the freedom and flexibility to choose how I spent my days and hours without having to consider the time I needed to dedicate to a nine-to-five, yet I still felt trapped by a system of labor and capitalism and was burning myself out because I feared not being productive. But honestly, I did not know what life was like outside of productivity, doing and keeping busy, and this brought me to a deep realization: As much as I talked about wanting rest, I had no clue what rest was outside of sleep. Many of us believe rest is taking a nap and getting six to eight hours of sleep every night, but there is more to it than just our sleep habits, and the system of toxic productivity is constantly disrupting it. Before unpacking the meaning of rest and how to tap into it, let's unpack toxic productivity.

When Productivity Becomes Toxic— and the Need for Boundaries

There is nothing wrong with wanting to be productive. Merriam-Webster defines the word "productive" in the following ways: (1) having the quality or power of producing especially in abundance, (2) effective in bringing about, and (3) yielding results, benefits, and profits. When we want things in life, we must be productive in the process of bringing about and yielding results. To write this book, I had to carve space out of my day to do research, read books on creativity, make room for writer's block, and most important, write. I had to be productive in those areas to bring forth this book you are currently reading. There were times during this process, however, when I was engaging in toxic productivity, which simply means engaging in excessive doing and constantly being busy without periods of breaks or rest, which causes stress and burnout. To be precise, while writing this book, I ebbed and flowed between healthy productivity and toxic productivity. Anytime I found myself engaging in rest, I would think in the back of my head, "The book isn't going to write itself," and immediately I would abandon whatever I was doing to get back to writing. There were days when I would operate off one meal because I was too busy writing to cook, or I'd be up all night with fire-red eyes refusing to close my laptop because the thought of not writing made me feel not only anxious but lazy. I kept telling myself I had no excuses for not making progress, and I punched down on myself whenever I took moments away from writing to either hang out and socialize or even lounge around and watch Netflix.

All my life, all I've ever known was engaging in productivity to escape myself; it's why school was always so important to me. It was a distraction from being with myself. Then when I graduated, I quickly entered the workforce to not have to spend time alone with myself. And now here I was, an entrepreneur who had the privilege to make space for more downtime, rest, and disengaging, and instead I was on 24-7 and beating myself up for being exhausted. Learning to disconnect from the culture of excessive doing and toxic productivity is seriously a day-by-day, moment-by-moment task. It requires mindfulness and a willingness to do something different, no matter how uncomfortable it feels. Hustle culture tells us to be on, ready, and available at all times through the day, and this mindset is why urgency culture is so prevalent and a lack of boundaries is such a societal norm. Too many of us have forgotten how to hold space for pause. If we call someone, we feel anxious and like a burden if they don't answer. If we ask someone to hang out and they decline, we create a negative narrative about them not wanting to hang out with us instead of honoring a person's need for rest and disconnection, which has nothing to do with us, yet we take things personally and make everything about us.

> Too many of us have forgotten how to hold space for pause.

Toxic productivity is deeply rooted in a culture of poor boundaries. A lot of people have been taught that niceness means self-abandonment. I should not be expected to harm myself to make someone feel good or have their needs met. It's why it's always important to assess what we say yes to, because too often, we find ourselves saying yes because we are committed to the person making the request, instead of assessing whether we have the capacity to be committed to the task they're asking of us. I can love you and say no. I can love you and decline your phone call. I can love you and not have the energetic capacity to engage with you. I can love you and love myself at the same time.

Our desire to please and be everything to everyone, while also having people view us a superhumans with capes, is why the act of resting can feel so difficult, because when you choose rest, you are choosing to put the cape away and be unavailable. But if you find your worth only in what you do for others, you will never rest. Resting requires us to say no, but if you are eager to please and fear disappointing people, you will not rest; you will burn yourself out. Resting asks us to do less and take breaks, but if you find your worth in your accolades, job promotions, and titles, you will exhaust yourself until your death, and your titles, degrees, and rewards will have no value to you then. Most important, rest asks us to make time, but we refuse to, so we fill our calendars with things that keep us busy, and even when we have downtime, we misdirect our energy toward things that don't rejuvenate us. When I listen to the reasons people struggle to rest, a few myths about the concept of rest generally come up.

Myth #1: Rest Requires Balance

You cannot give everything in your life equal attention. By trying to do so, you will become drained and burned out. It's why the concept of work-life balance is a facade. The scales are never even. The word "balance" means to give something equal distribution, and what this tells me is that if we are seeking balance in life, we are not being wise with identifying our priorities. Everything you do does not require equal energy. Checking emails, for example, should not require the same amount of energy as working on a project with a next-day deadline. If you are trying to give equal effort to everything in front of you, then you are neglecting something in return. Growing up, I used to have an AT&T cell phone plan that came with rollover minutes. Every month, whatever minutes I did not use got rolled over into the next payment cycle, which helped me gain more minutes. Every now and then, I think we try to approach time in this manner and trick ourselves into believing that time will roll over into the next day so that we can aim to balance it all, when ultimately, time restarts itself daily and what you have time for today you may not have time for tomorrow—and there will be no rollover minutes for you to claim. Balance is not a requirement for rest, but mindfulness is. When you practice mindfulness, you can be more in tune with the things that matter and distribute your time in a way that brings harmony to your life. Be mindful and intentional about your time because you do not get refunds when it comes to how you spend your energy.

Myth #2: Rest Means Getting a Lot of Sleep

I know many people who get a full six to eight hours of sleep, yet throughout the day they are still drained, exhausted, and tired. Sleep is extremely important for your mental health, so I am not diminishing that as a practice for rest, but rest does not start when you get in bed at night and end when your morning alarm clock goes off. Rest begins when you are intentional about having a nighttime routine that increases your quality of sleep. It's worth exploring the different forms of disruption you carry into your bedroom. Is it your phone in your hand? Anger from unresolved conflict? The scent of a long, exhausting day? Anxiety from catastrophic thinking and scenarios in your head that are completely made up? Sometimes the energy we get in bed with can impact our ability to get the quality sleep we need. Being mindful about rest during the night can look like putting your phone on Do Not Disturb to do things like read a book, spend time with your partner, or simply put your mind at ease without added distractions. Rest before bed can also look like spending time journaling out the thoughts that are making you anxious or have you feeling angry, bitter, or resentful. It's finding ways to redirect that heavy energy outside your body and toward something more productive and beneficial to your mental health.

Myth #3: Rest Is Robbing You of Time You Can't Get Back

During my years in graduate school, I would always be so tired from school and my internship that whenever I had downtime, I fought with myself on whether I should use that time to study or take a nap. I would always choose the former, and while trying to study, I would be distracted, irritable, and most important, I never really retained much of the information I was exposing myself to because I was extremely tired. We have tricked ourselves into believing that rest is so unimportant that it is a setback to our ability to be productive, successful, and meet our goals, when in fact, rest is one of the most important tools for getting us closer to the things we are trying to achieve. *The time you spend resting isn't time wasted.* It is time that allows your brain to gain the optimal energy it needs to help you perform. Our brains need time to recuperate, so when we don't allow ourselves to rest, the brain's neurons become overworked, making it difficult for the brain to tap into stored information that we need for healthy decision-making, managing stress, and achieving optimal cognitive functioning.

Another important element of our cognitive wellness that gets impacted is our executive functioning skills, which include the following eight domains: working memory, self-monitoring, impulse control, emotional control, flexible thinking, planning and prioritizing, task initiation, and organization. When you look at this list, I am sure you can think of many areas of your life where you tap into all eight of these domains to either complete your workday or fulfill other tasks and responsibilities, so to think that rest is not beneficial to the brain and body and that it does not help you meet your goals would be injurious to your mental health and ability to thrive. You are not robbing yourself of time unless you use your time without wisdom and discernment.

Knowing the Kind of Rest You Need

Now that we've knocked out some myths that have kept us stuck and avoiding the essential elements of rest, let's unpack what rest even is. During her TED talk, physician Saundra Dalton-Smith, MD, shares that there are seven different types of rest, and sleep is only one element of those seven. When we consider these seven types of rest, we can understand what depletes us of our energy and discern what we need to rejuvenate and restore those areas.

1. **Physical rest (passive or active):** Our bodies store so much, including the stress and trauma that we carry, so giving the body the ability to rest and recuperate is essential for your emotional and mental well-being. Passive rest is where sleep comes in, and it helps us with calming those neurons in the brain and restoring the body. Active rest, however, is when we engage in somatic practices to alleviate the body of the heaviness it carries. Light exercise and yoga, and even holistic practices like physical therapy and getting massages, can fall into this category.

2. **Mental rest:** This form of rest can be important for people who struggle with anxiety and depression or have ruminating thoughts that they just can't seem to shut off. When we are struggling with mental deficits, our executive functioning skills are impacted, which is why so many people struggle with decision fatigue; they feel overloaded mentally and overwhelmed. To combat this, it's important to take mental breaks from stimuli that induce feelings of overwhelm and require high levels of processing. The chunking method is a great way to take mental breaks. You simply group tasks and to-do items that fit within a similar category so that your brain is not constantly overworked and trying to find ways to complete a task. For example, if you go to the grocery store, you would create a shopping list

and "chunk" together items that you would find in the same aisle. A work-related example would be batching tasks in numbers, such as checking ten emails, writing ten progress notes, completing ten pieces of paperwork—sticking to ten items at a time so as not to overexert yourself on a task that has the potential to become draining.

Another form of mental rest could look like dumping— which literally means dumping your mind of its thoughts. You can do this by writing your thoughts out in a journal or using the voice note app on your phone and talking out loud, even if it's to yourself. Last, when doing a very difficult task, mental rest can look like exposing yourself to stimuli that create a sense of ease. If you have been writing a difficult paper or essay, after ninety minutes you might take ten to fifteen minutes to do a meditation, stretch, or go for a walk before returning to the difficult stimulus.

3. **Sensory rest:** We were not created to sit in front of a brightly lit computer screen for eight hours a day. We are also not wired to stare at our phones all day. Did you know that the average American checks their phone 344 times a day, which equates to once every four minutes? How many times did you glance at your phone while trying to get through this chapter? We are so connected and attached to our devices that we don't even realize a lot of our fatigue and exhaustion come from sensory overload. We must stop treating our brains like they are machines. Finally commit to closing the fifty tabs you have open on your

computer, and come to terms with the fact that you are never going to revisit those web pages.

I have a motto that I use to alert myself that I am doing too much: "Stop doing dishes in your bedroom." One day I decided to play robot and started multitasking while simultaneously washing the dishes. I went to sit and watch TV, and when I was done, I noticed I couldn't find the remote. I searched endlessly and remembered the last place I had been was the kitchen. I thought it was a bizarre place to check for my remote, but something nudged me to open the kitchen cabinet, and lo and behold, there sat my remote. But then I realized two of my mugs were missing, so I backtracked and remembered that after I left the kitchen I went into my bedroom. Lo and behold, my cleaned mugs were sitting on my bed. I of course laughed at myself and took that time to realize my brain was way too overstimulated, and I thought this must be a live enactment of what it looks like to mentally crash. **Learn to disconnect.** If you experience sensory overload from being in loud environments, try working with noise cancellation headphones. If you are constantly in front of a computer screen, take moments of rest by closing your eyes and visualizing something that is calming. If you spend most of your day on Zoom calls, during the breaks you have, close your laptop and fixate on something in your environment to help you feel grounded; maybe focus on your plants or an object in front of you. If you find that being overloaded during the day impacts your ability to sleep at night, try sleeping with an eye mask or weighted blanket to help regulate your nervous system and put it into rest mode.

4. **Creative rest:** As a business owner, I wear many hats. I'm a writer, public speaker, mental health consultant, and wellness coach. During moments of high stress, I'd sometimes think to myself, *I wish I had a mindless job.* Having to always create, problem-solve, research, and brainstorm new ideas and concepts would feel draining for me at times, and I just wanted to shut my brain off for a day and make it all stop. This made me realize that I was experiencing creative overload and not giving myself the space I needed to tap into play and enjoy mindless activities. Creative rest is giving yourself permission to take a break from all the mind-boggling work you do and lean into the arts, nature, and other things that invoke feelings of awe and wonder and deepen your creative potential. As a writer, sometimes I need to take creative breaks that include visiting museums or even traveling as a way to expose myself to things I've never seen or experienced before, and it does help awaken my creative potential.

   Another way to tap into creative rest is through music and live performances. Although I have never gone to see a live orchestra, I'm a big fan of listening to classical music, because I can focus on the sound of the instruments rather than reciting and listening to lyrics. Find ways to increase your sense of play and wonder when you feel mentally taxed out. There is so much to see, do, and experience in life, and when we exert all our energy in fulfilling tasks, we deplete ourselves of the energy needed to care for ourselves in ways that are detached from the constant cycle of busyness and work. Play will always be central to who we are, even as adults, and instead of putting it on the back burner, we must to reframe the way we see play and creativity and how they are a vital part in enhancing our well-being.

5. **Spiritual rest:** So much of life exists outside ourselves, which is why belonging, connection, and community are so important. They play a role in enhancing our spiritual well-being and remind us of the things that truly matter in life. Earlier I talked about the movie *Soul*. For the character Joe, it took spiritual rest in the form of death to help him understand his passion and purpose in life. He had to step away from himself and his ego to see the world and his life through a lens of what it means to be connected to others, while simultaneously enjoying life on a moment-by-moment basis, versus enjoying only the things he deemed an accomplishment. Luckily for us, we can lean into spiritual rest without having to experience death like Joe did. For some, spiritual rest might look like cultivating a relationship with a higher power such as God, having faith as one navigates the world through prayer, and being intentional about living in alignment with God. For others, spiritual rest might look like disconnecting from distractions and people and having moments of solitude to connect with yourself or with what's happening around you on a deeper level. It's why wellness re-

treats are so popular. They create a space that allows us to step away from busyness and connect to something greater, whether it be God, ourselves, or the community of people we are surrounded by. On a cultural level, I think of the ways food is spiritual in my Panamanian household. There is something special about the ability to bond over food and how gatherings bring people together. Being offered a plate of food is like an invitation, a welcoming into the family and into this community. Culturally, we all have spiritual practices we may have learned from our ancestors or have cultivated for ourselves today that are not traditionally honored in American society, but I urge you to reconnect with the things that once played a role in providing you safety, connection, and refuge.

6. **Emotional rest:** A culture of busyness has forced us to learn how to compartmentalize to care for the many responsibilities that we must show up for and tend to. We don't always have the space to process our feelings and the things that invoke them because life keeps moving forward and we can't risk falling behind, forcing us to play catch-up. But when we keep going and going, sometimes we neglect ourselves and the things we need for our emotional healing. Urgency culture, including the inability to resist it, breeds a culture of people pleasers and folks with poor boundaries. Emotional rest requires introspection and self-awareness. It requires asking ourselves, "Do I have the energetic capacity to take on more right now? Do I even want to do what is being asked of me? Do I need a moment of pause before giving a

response?" When we practice emotional rest, we resist the culture of burnout and constantly overwhelming ourselves with tasks and responsibilities that we know we cannot, or do not want to, fulfill. Getting better with your boundaries is the only way to ensure you are practicing emotional rest. Often, tendencies like people-pleasing are a coping mechanism to either deal with or avoid conflict and tension, but the result is always self-injurious.

When we people-please, we are disconnected from ourselves in the moment and trying to become more in tune with fixing the feelings of others, instead of identifying what we feel and what we need for our own emotional safety and refuge. Another reason why we people-please is because we have been taught to abandon ourselves to care for the needs of others. This can happen if you grew up parentified and had to play the role of caretaker very early on in life. You may have made being a helper your core identity and find gratification in being able to serve others, and although there is nothing wrong with being generous, it is important to make sure that your kindness to others does not result in harm toward yourself, because that is not kindness but self-sabotage.

I encourage you to begin by setting boundaries with yourself. What are some things you give your time to that you can start saying no to? It might be watching less TV, scrolling on social media less, shopping less, or saying no to distractions that get in the way of you being your healthiest self. Learning to set boundaries with ourselves teaches us that we can handle discomfort, and when we learn that it is possible for us to work through our hard emotions, we also learn that it is possible for others to handle the disappointment of hearing no and that we are not responsible for or obligated to do their healing work.

PRACTICE SAYING THESE THINGS TO GAIN EMOTIONAL REST:

- "I would love to help, but I currently do not have the emotional capacity and I don't want to give you half of myself. I will be sure to circle back with you when the time is right."

- "I appreciate the invite, but I won't be able to attend. I'm grateful that you thought of me, though."

- "I'm so happy you got to come over and that we could spend time together. I feel myself becoming drowsy now, so I will have to wrap up our time together, but thank you again for visiting."

- "I'm honestly not the right person to help with this. I don't want to misinform you, so I think you are better off seeking assistance from someone with more knowledge about this."

- "I appreciate you wanting to come by, but I'm not up for visitors at the moment. I will circle back, however, and let you know when it's a good time to visit."

7. **Social rest:** This form of rest can be directly correlated with emotional rest. During Dr. Dalton-Smith's talk, she states, "An emotional rest deficit and a social rest deficit often coexist.

This happens when we fail to differentiate between those relationships that revive us from those relationships that exhaust us." There is a strong correlation between who we surround ourselves with and their impact on our well-being. It's important to surround yourself with people who are supportive, emotionally safe, and who cultivate a space of acceptance and belonging, but what's also critical to understand is that we can feel drained even when we are around people who are good for us. I had a client once tell me that whenever a particular friend came over, she always felt exhausted after they left, although she enjoyed their company, and she didn't feel this way regarding other very close friends in her life. One of the things my client learned was the differentiation between acquaintances and friends, and the kind of friends we regard as family. Whenever this particular friend visited, my client would always ensure a meal was cooked, her house was super clean, and she was as hospitable as can be, since it was a new connection and she wanted this person to feel welcome. However, whenever her best friend, who was like family, was at her house, she didn't have to do the work of prepping a meal or tidying up because she felt like she could be the messy version of herself. That meant most house rules didn't apply to them. If this person was hungry, they were welcome to go into the fridge and grab something, versus the acquaintance friend who she felt she had to serve. When her best friend was over, it was easy to do things like watching TV or not filling the space with conversation, versus feeling the need to entertain and not bore her houseguest when her acquaintance friend was over.

I informed my client that she might not have the energetic capacity at times to have her acquaintance friend over to her home because of the labor it requires, which disrupts her ability to feel at ease, and suggested that instead of inviting this friend to her home, she could choose to meet up at a restaurant where they both would be served and my client would not have to worry about doing all the serving, entertaining, and performing. She got to feel like a guest, too, instead of being a host.

People who are introverted can also benefit from this differentiation. Introverts often turn inward to stimulate themselves versus seeking external validation. Disconnecting is a key trait of an introverted person, but I've often had introverts ask me what they can do to ensure that their disconnection from others does not turn into isolation. A key way to prevent this from happening is by surrounding yourself with people who give you the space to turn inward even while in their presence. This can look like being around other introverts who understand when you go quiet, become less talkative, or even decide you've had enough fun at the gathering and choose to go home. These are people who don't take your disconnecting personally and understand your need for restoration and recharging, which allows for social rest without the burden of explaining or trying to get people to understand your personality type.

Another form of social rest we need is learning to disconnect from the interactions that come our way through our devices. During the early stages of the coronavirus pandemic, many people began to complain about Zoom fatigue, as well as the constant phone calls and text messages they were being inundated with because of the inability to engage in in-person interactions. Even virtually, we can become drained when we are expected to always be available, and our devices do not help because we can always be reached. One of my favorite hacks is putting my phone on Do Not Disturb even when I am doing absolutely nothing, because even during my downtime I can acknowledge that having a phone call or texting repeatedly is a form of energetic labor and increases sensory overload. When a person is not available, it can be for all sorts of reasons, and we must stop guilt-tripping people for not being free to fulfill our desires. We also must stop guilt-tripping ourselves for not having the emotional and energetic capacity to always show up. If we want to honor our humanness, we must be willing to honor our limitations and recognize we are not wired to always be available and connected and running life on a hamster wheel without giving ourselves a break and the rest we deserve to show up as the best version for ourselves.

Ultimately, rest is vital for our health in many ways, and it's important to begin expanding our ideas and definition of rest. I know that we are all busy and have a list of responsibilities we must tend to, but rest doesn't happen by accident. It is intentional and happens when we make time and put in effort. Stop putting limitations on what you think rest is, open your eyes to things that drain you, and find ways to preserve your energy.

- Learning to disengage from unhealthy conversations is a form of rest.
- Learning to be okay with not having the last word is a form of rest.

- Learning to mind your business is a form of rest.
- Learning to say no is a form of rest.
- Learning to ask for what you need instead of getting upset that others aren't reading your mind is a form of rest.

Easing into rest and breaking away from the norm of busyness and toxic productivity is a daily practice, so be gentle with yourself. It takes time to rewire the way we have been conditioned to view passion, purpose, fulfillment, and success, which are dimensions that traditionally require us to stay busy, always be on, and be on demand to perform labor. The only way to create a new narrative around rest, purpose, and the American dream is to live in alignment with the truth you define for yourself—not society's truths, but your truth. Begin thinking about what it means to live a full life outside of the labor you perform by using the following exercises to reflect:

Exercise, Part One

- In your own words, how do you define the American dream? (Feel free to answer this even if you live in a different country.)
- What myths do you need to let go of when you think about what it means to be successful?
- How has trying to be successful increased feelings of stress, anxiety, and burnout in your life? And what do you need to do differently to create space for healing, rest, and ease?

- Think of social capital, and name three people who are important members of your supportive circle. If you do not have anyone you can name, what has stood in the way of you building social connections?
- What have you been taught about community and what it means to build healthy friendships, connections, and social networks?

Exercise, Part Two

Write out three ways you will practice the seven dimensions of rest.

PHYSICAL (ACTIVE AND PASSIVE):

1. _____

2. _____

3. _____

MENTAL:

1. _____

2. _____

3. _____

SENSORY:

1. _____

2. _____

3. _____

CREATIVE:

1. _____

2. _____

3. _____

SPIRITUAL:

1. _____

2. _____

3. _____

EMOTIONAL:

1. _____

2. _____

3. _____

SOCIAL:

1. _____

2. _____

3. _____

— 7 —

THE STRUGGLE OF BEING HUMAN

Tips, Tools, and Practices
for Living a Full, Whole Life

Now that you've made it this far into the book, you've learned a lot about a variety of things, including hard truths, and it can be hard to take it all in at once—so don't. The beautiful thing about books is that you have the ability to revisit the material from time to time. You may have chosen to read this book from front to back, back to front, or starting with whatever chapter seemed most appealing to you. You may also have found yourself not wanting to read the book anymore at all (but maybe you did if you made it this far) because you realize the content in this book is not for you, and that is okay too. Regardless of the journey it took to make it to this chapter, I'm glad that you're here. Healing is in itself a journey, and it takes time to do the work of repairing and nourishing your soul, growing and elevating, managing your traumas, and learning to tolerate distress. It's important not to put too much pressure on yourself to be perfect and well put together because you will mess up and not always get things right the first try (or even the second or third).

The process of healing is a natural ebbing and flowing of ups and downs, grief and gratitude, joy and sorrow, and—I've mentioned this in previous chapters—learning and unlearning. As you move on from this book, remember that you have a full, wonderful, and whole life to live. Don't be afraid to take a chance on yourself, try new things, make new friends, or find a partner because you are so fixated on healing. Remember that healing happens best in community. Healing happens when we give ourselves permission to experience life and learn lessons along the way. I wish I could give you the option of purchasing a remedy that will always make you feel better, but I cannot because that item does not exist. This is also why we are such a consumer-based society; we like convenience and quick fixes. We are impatient with ourselves, with our pain, our anger, and our sadness. We are quick to buy the things that are sold to us because of the promise that they will make life less difficult and even more fulfilling.

Take a moment to pause and look at your bookshelf or library. How many books do you possess on the topic of self-help that have been left untouched? How many unused journals do you have sitting in a drawer, but you keep buying more because they're pretty and appealing? What would it look like to challenge yourself to believe that you do not need to do more or possess more, that you are right where you need to be, and that you have permission to enter a season of slowness and steadiness instead of adding more to your plate because you think it'll make you spotless, perfect, or happy? You can have all the tools, techniques, and healing manuals at your disposal and still make mistakes that impact your growth. You can have all the knowledge and information to do better and still struggle with turning that information into action. It's important that you find ways to honor the fact that you are human and not an emotionless robot or machine. I understand it's hard to live in a space where your emotions are heavy, and you are tired of grieving, crying, and being triggered, but I need you to trust that your feelings do not define the totality of your life. What you feel in a moment is fleeting. It is not forever. Find the courage to release the idea that hardships are what you are destined for and learn to make space for joy, gratitude, and love as a remedy for healing.

Long before I was Minaa B. to the public, I was simply a young girl turned woman who had dreams and aspirations and felt inadequate for not being where she thought she should have been in life. I would punch down on myself consistently for not having more, being more, or doing more. Even when I was doing to the point where I couldn't exert any more energy to even sustain myself, I was still self-critical for not meeting certain milestones. It didn't help that I was comparing myself to my peers or even strangers on the internet. I adopted all the life hacks: wake up early, work out, read all the books, buy a planner, write in a journal, organize your closet, be this and do that, yet I still held on to this belief that I was so far behind. All this self-improvement work was just turning into self-shaming work. These habits can be extremely useful to some, but when they are not and when they feel like another joyless task to check off the to-do list, then at some point you must be willing to slow down and assess the ways you might be pursuing perfection over wholeness.

In the slowing down, you might notice how you are doing all this work to be busy to avoid yourself or something deeper, or maybe you are trying to keep up with someone else you have no business trying to compete with. You might even notice whether it's your way of trying to resist being oppressed by stereotypes and feeling the need to perform to appeal to certain people or be seen as enough. My life started to align with my goals and vision for myself when I decided to define happiness on my own terms and find what motivated me to get out of bed every morning. I really needed to dig deep and understand what gave my life value and meaning, and I had to cultivate the courage to step outside my comfort zone to give myself the life I felt I deserved to have. Courage isn't something that just falls into our laps; it's something that we build, brick by brick, and one step at a time. The more you do this work, the more you may notice the dance between grief and growth. We do not evolve without having to go through transition and loss. Healing is a deeply complex experience because reality is hard to face sometimes, and we find ourselves playing tug-of-war with denial and truth. In the end, acknowledging and accepting truth is what brings us closer to ourselves. Don't fight change when it approaches. Do the uncomfortable work of leaning into it. Limiting ourselves to just one way of being is how we stifle our growth, and it puts blinkers over our eyes that stop us from seeing the different ways purpose and meaning can manifest day-to-day.

As you do this work of healing, growing, and evolving, it's important that you teach yourself how to cope with difficulty and adversity. Healing does not stop pain from existing, but it does give us the tolerance to manage our pain when we have the tools needed to regulate it by using the brain and body. I've compiled a list of tools, reminders, and practices for you to engage in to help you on your healing journey ahead. Come back to this chapter time and time again when you feel you are uneasy, triggered, or activated and need tools and reminders to get you through the moment.

Reminders About Growth and Self-Care

- You are allowed to take care of yourself and be your priority. You don't have to wait until you are struggling, exhausted, or burned out to tend to your well-being. Self-care is a prevention strategy, not just a crisis response.

- Sometimes you can play a role in your own suffering by standing by waiting for other people to change, instead of being accountable and deciding what you will no longer tolerate. Remember that you have to be an active participant in creating the change you seek in your life.

- Pick the people who you give your energy to wisely. Remember that checklist items like looks, education, social status, income, etc., do not correlate with being emotionally mature, available, or intelligent. The quality of your relationships will impact your mental health.

- When you are the person who wants to break generational dysfunction, erect boundaries, and protect your peace, you will often be chastised, ostracized, and mislabeled as problematic. Healing will often come with a challenge. Keep pushing forward anyway.

- You probably already have all the coping skills you need, and yet there are some things in life that are hard to cope with. Some things just require time, space, and acceptance in order for you to heal.

- Growth requires us to leave something behind. It may be our habits, beliefs, career, and even certain people. This is why making space for grief in the midst of growth is important. You have to mourn your former life to make space for a newer you.

- There are going to be days when self-care means allowing yourself to be angry, annoyed, and even isolated. Sometimes you won't care to do "the work," and you don't have to feel guilty about it. We all have these moments. Feel it and let it pass. Allow yourself to be human.

- Progress is the result of consistency. What's never been done before will always be hard the first time, but "firsts" are a necessary part of life. Challenge yourself to do the things you've been putting off and remember that perfectionism leads to inaction. Do and learn as you go.

• You can be doing the work and still have hard days, feel deep sadness, lack self-trust, and miss red flags. Growth is a daily practice; show yourself grace.

Reminders About Relationships

• The quality of your relationships matters. Whether it be a friend, parent, family member, or a partner, the people you surround yourself with can impact your mental health. Stop feeling obligated to be around people who are familiar but detrimental to your well-being.

• Sometimes the people you are seeking support from may be unequipped to give you what you need. Remember that two things can be true at once: someone being unequipped to hold space for you can also be someone who deeply loves you and wants the best for you.

• Living a full, abundant life will require you to be okay with disappointing people. Some people will have opinions regarding what they think is right for you and will expect you to abide by them, but your life is yours to live. You get to decide what is for you and what is not.

• Stop expecting people to know what you're thinking, feeling, or need from your tone, mood, or energy. Signs can be misinterpreted, and people cannot respond to what they don't know is being said. Be willing to express yourself clearly and directly. It's okay to speak up!

- Missing someone is not an indicator that they belong in your life. You can miss someone and process the grief of no longer being connected to them without trying to invite them back in. Moving on is possible by creating your own closure.

- Love and struggle do not have to coexist. You are deserving of love that is clear and kind and rooted in peace and not confusion. Chaos and dysfunction do not have to be the prerequisites to healthy commitment.

- You do not have to be the strong friend or family figure all the time. It's okay to allow life to unfold without stepping in to save others when you are also in need of saving. Caring for others more than you care for yourself does more harm than good to your relationships.

- Normalize selective sharing. Everyone you know does not have to be in your business. Privacy and secrecy are not the same. You are the one who is in control of choosing who has access to you and your personal information. Discern wisely.

Reminders About Boundaries

- Please recognize that "I don't want to" is a very clear boundary and another way of saying no. It is not an invitation for you to try to change someone's mind.

- Stop telling people "It's okay" when it's not. Stop telling people "I will think about it" when you already know the answer. Stop telling people yes when you want to say no. Stop self-betraying by being passive, and instead start taking ownership by being assertive.

- You're probably aware that if you set a boundary, the whole dynamic of your relationship will change, maybe even fall apart. It's okay if you're not ready yet. Your window of tolerance will alert you when you can't continue on this way anymore.

- You can have compassion for people, their struggles, and their trauma, and you can also have boundaries and safeguard yourself from people who cause you harm and abuse due to their trauma. Regardless of what we've gone through, we are all responsible for healing ourselves.

- When erecting boundaries with harmful people, there might be times when you have to resort to avoidance or ghosting in order to protect yourself from harm. When other people refuse to respect your boundaries, you have to know when it's time to disengage.

• You cannot control how people respond to your boundaries. Their disappointment, anger, or hurt is not an indication that your boundary is inappropriate; it's simply a reflection of how they are feeling, and it is their responsibility to tend to their feelings.

Meditation Practices

Meditation and deep-breathing exercises are great for managing stress, anxiety, and trauma responses such as fight, flight, freeze, and fawning. A myth about meditation is that your mind must be completely turned off or else you are not doing the practice right. That is not the case. It's okay if your mind wanders. During those wandering moments, you can focus on your breaths. Another thing to consider is maybe your mind is wandering toward places that need your attention and that you've been deflecting or avoiding. Either way, there are many effective ways to practice this skill for your mental health.

• **Guided Meditation:** If you enjoy meditating to someone's words and receiving instructional cues on what to focus on for mind-body alignment, this form of meditation can be helpful. The best way to access this type of meditation is to visit the app store on your phone and see what is available to you. Calm, Head-space, and BetterSleep are great apps that offer guided medita-tions.

- **Rainbow Breathing:** During this form of meditation, you will focus on your breaths by inhaling for four counts, then exhaling for four. The goal is to visualize the colors of the rainbow as you inhale, and then imagine the colors fading away as you exhale. Repeat until you feel calm and centered.

- **Visualization:** Rainbow breathing is a great example of visual-ization. Visualization is when you focus on imagery to increase your focus and induce mindfulness. During this practice, you can inhale for four counts, then exhale for four. As you focus on your breaths, begin to imagine a person, place, or thing—real or imagined, whether from a dream or a TV show that you watched. Visualize yourself in this space as if it were real life happen-ing around you. You can do this by engaging your five senses as you continue to focus on your breaths and the imagery you cre-ated. What do you smell? What do you hear? What do you taste? What do you feel? What do you see? Repeat until you feel calm and centered.

- **Loving-Kindness Meditation:** If you are currently in conflict with someone you love, such as a partner, friend, or family mem-ber, this kind of meditation practice can help with repairing rup-tures and cultivating healing. During the meditation you will focus on your breathing, inhaling for four counts and exhaling for four. As you do this, begin to focus your attention on the person with whom you are seeking to repair a rupture or make amends. Begin to say out loud affirmations of love, empathy, and kindness for that person. Name qualities that you like about them, including elements of their character and personality. The goal of this meditation is to exert positive and loving energy toward others and to fill yourself with kind thoughts, which are often filtered out when we are angry or in conflict with someone.

• **Body Scan:** This is one of my favorite meditations for holistic healing and releasing trauma trapped in the body that manifests as muscle aches, tension, and other aches and chronic pain. It also helps reduce stress and improve sleep. To do this practice, you want to ensure you are in a comfortable position, such as sitting in a chair or lying down flat. You will begin to breathe into your belly and focus on your breaths, inhaling and exhaling for four counts. Now become aware of your body, starting from your toes or feet and slowly making your way up to the top of your head. During this process, as you move from one body part to the next, pay attention to the sensations you feel. It can be pain, tension, or an ache; pause there and begin to breathe through it. Depending on the area of the body, you can also move it slowly as you breathe, so if you are feeling pain in your foot, you may rotate your foot clockwise, then counterclockwise, as you inhale and exhale. You can also do this to the neck or wrist area to help take stress off those often-painful areas.

Grounding Practices

Grounding techniques are practices beneficial for cultivating mindfulness when you are feeling triggered, anxious, or having panic attacks. These practices can be used to manage distress, increase your mood, and center you when you are dissociating.

- **5-4-3-2-1 Method:** This popular technique is a simple way to regulate your body when you are experiencing distressing feelings and thoughts. You engage your five senses in the following ways. Name five things you can see, four things that you can hear, three things that you can feel, two things that you can smell, and one thing that you can taste. If you feel like this may be too overstimulating for you, focus on one thing instead for each of your five senses.

- **Cold Shower or Ice Bath:** Regulating your body's temperature when you are feeling anxious or triggered can help calm your nervous system. Ice baths, cold showers, or even running your hands under cold water or splashing some on your face can help with activating the sympathetic nervous system, which controls the fight-or-flight response, and putting the body in recovery mode.

- **Calm Music:** Another way to ground yourself is through music that is calming and helps you feel centered. Many of us have easy access to music libraries on our phones, which we carry everywhere with us; a pair of headphones can be a great tool when you are in a public setting or overwhelmed in a social crowd and need to find a way to regulate yourself. Consider classical musical or instrumentals when you are dealing with sensory overload or anxiety, or soft, calming music to help put you at ease. Binaural music is also a therapeutically designed form of meditative music that helps slow down a speedy heart rate, regulate your nervous system, and promote slower breathing. You can find this kind of music on YouTube, Spotify, and other streaming music platforms.

- **Sound Awareness:** This practice is simple. You listen to the sounds and noises that exist around you to help you disengage from the thoughts you are having in your head or the triggers you feel being activated in your body. Simply focus your energy outward and start to fixate on the things you hear. Begin to breathe as you focus your attention on the sounds. Do you hear birds chirping? Cars humming? A baby crying? People talking—what are they saying? When we tune into the world around us, we remind ourselves to be rooted back into reality, and we pull ourselves out of the past or the anxious places our anxiety takes us to.

- **Self-Compassion Affirmations:** When experiencing, anxiety, depression, or a deeply debilitating experience, you may use negative self-talk to teach yourself to cope through self-blame and judgment. However, self-deprecation does not help us heal our wounds. In fact, it makes them more fragile. Self-compassion is vital for our healing, so when we feel dysregulated by negative thoughts, begin repeating positive affirmations out loud so that you can rewire those negative thoughts. Affirmations can include:

- "I am still worthy of care and love, even when I mess up."
- "I made a mistake, but I am not a failure."
- "I am doing my best with the skills I have. I am enough."
- "I am not defined by my pain; I can move past this feeling."

- **Tune Into Nature:** Our environment has tools for our healing, which is a beautiful gift from the earth to us. Exposure to nature has both psychological and physiological benefits. It helps reduce stress, boost your mood, and improve cognitive functioning like working memory and increased attention. When stress is regulated, the body experiences more benefits, including for the immune system, blood pressure, and more. Tuning into nature can look like listening to sounds such as the rain or birds chirping. It can also look like visiting a park, going on a hike, or tending to your own plants, which can be beneficial for your mental health.

Journaling Prompts and Practices

Every day our minds are filled with information, thoughts, memories, and so forth, and learning to tune these things out and be more present can be difficult. Journaling as a practice for healing the mind can be beneficial when dealing with depression, anxiety, PTSD, and life in general, because you don't need to have a diagnosis to feel pain or go through hardship. Journaling can be a difficult practice for some, but I encourage you not to put too much thought into it. This is not a college essay assignment or a dissertation. This is simply words on paper that you have full control over and do not need to go through an editing process. Journaling has been proven to help with achieving goals, reducing stress, boosting your mood, and managing triggers. Here are some ways that you can begin practicing journaling for your well-being:

- **Free-Flow Journaling:** This practice is very straightforward. You write out whatever thoughts are coming to mind. You can write about what you had for lunch, how you felt when you woke up, the person who pissed you off, or anything that is currently taking up space within your mind.

- **Gratitude Journaling:** This form of journaling is specifically about focusing on the things you are grateful for. Life can feel overwhelmingly heavy, and when adversity arises, it can distract us from the things that are going well. When you are feeling anxiety about the future or outcomes that you cannot control, gratitude helps you refocus your attention on the things you can control and your positive experiences. A gratitude practice to start doing is an exercise called Three Good Things. As you wind down at the end of your day, reflect and name three good things that happened to you today and what were the particular details that made them good.

- **Affirmation Journaling:** Building confidence and boosting your self-esteem require positive self-talk. You can engage in this practice by writing out positive messages about yourself, both real and imagined. It can feel hard to write down things that you don't believe about yourself, but the more you write out these truths, the more you will begin to live in alignment with them and make them your reality. A simple positive thought and shift in mindset can boost your mood and self-esteem.

- **Goal-Setting Journaling:** Having goals in life helps us with learning and unlearning because goals help us identify new behaviors we want to develop and barriers that stand in the way. Sometimes a barrier can be a mental block, and sometimes it can be a more tangible issue. The best way to set goals is to use the SMART Method to ensure you are creating goals that are realistic and measurable.
  - **Specific:** Try to avoid being vague and get as specific as possible when creating a goal.
  - **Measurable:** Describe the evidence that will help you recognize when you are moving in the right direction and making progress.
  - **Actionable:** What are the actual steps that you will engage in to meet this goal? Make sure you set realistic expectations.
  - **Relevant:** How is this goal in alignment with your values and the life you are trying to live currently?

- **Time-Based:** Create a realistic time frame for when you would like to achieve this goal. Be willing to move the goalpost if needed.

- **Dear Self Letters:** Writing yourself a letter can feel cathartic, and it is a spiritual practice that can help with letting go. Simply start off your letter with *Dear Self,* and write the things you've been wanting to say to your current, past, or future self. Some prompts to help guide you can be:
  - Dear Self, I am forgiving myself for . . .
  - Dear Self, I am making space in my life for . . .
  - Dear Self, I am committed to giving myself more . . .
  - Dear Self, I will stop worrying about . . .

- **The Burn Box:** Sometimes you might find yourself wanting to release something and never look back. Write out whatever is on your heart and either burn it, trash it, or shred it. This journaling method is a cathartic practice of releasing and letting go, instead of holding on to what no longer serves you.

Brain Chemistry and Happiness Chemicals

Hormones are chemicals that get released in the body and travel through your bloodstream and act as messengers to help regulate your mood, sexual functioning, metabolism, and more. Poor hormone levels can have a great impact on both your mental and your physical health. The good thing is that there are natural ways to get your body to release more hormones—specifically, dopamine, serotonin, endorphins, and oxytocin, known as the happiness hormones.

- **Dopamine:** This hormone is known as the "feel-good" hormone. It plays a central role in inducing happiness and activating the brain's reward system. Tools to increase dopamine production include:
  - Watching comedic shows, movies, etc.
  - Traveling, sightseeing, or visiting a new environment
  - Trying new activities: painting, roller-skating, knitting, etc.

- **Serotonin:** This hormone helps with mood regulation, which is why it's known as the mood-boosting hormone. Tools to increase serotonin production include:
  - Getting adequate sleep
  - Meditation
  - Well-balanced meals
  - Spending time outdoors and in nature

- **Endorphins:** This hormone is known as the body's pain reliever and is highly linked to exercise practices, which help induce pleasure and relieve stress and pain. Tools for endorphin production include:
  - Exercise: high-intensity interval training, cardio, walking, yoga, stretching, Pilates, dance

- Rewatching old TV shows, listening to music that induces a positive memory, looking through an old photo album
- Cooking a meal, trying a new recipe, or eating nutritional foods

- **Oxytocin:** Known as the love hormone, oxytocin helps increase feelings of connection, intimacy, and bonding. Tools to increase oxytocin production include:
  - Physical intimacy: sex, kissing, cuddling, etc.
  - Emotional intimacy: bonding, quality time, words of affirmation, vulnerability
  - Touch: a handshake, a warm hug, an arm around a shoulder
  - Service work: volunteering, charity work, donating, etc.

Moving Forward with Self-Trust

One of the ultimate gifts we can give ourselves is trusting that we know what we need. This journey of healing will be long and will come with challenges, and when you face obstacles, it's okay to lean into your own wisdom and trust that you know what you need to feel safe, secure, and move forward.

We live in a loud world. One where we hear opinions daily from the people we know personally as well as on social media. Everywhere you turn, there is a voice that will try to tell you how to live, but one of the best ways to know you are healing is when you finally learn to trust your-self and your ability to make choices for your betterment, instead of second-guessing yourself and constantly requiring approval and valida-tion from others on whether your needs matter or how you should live your life. In order to put everything you've learned into practice, you must trust that you can harness the ability to discern what you need and find ways to provide it to yourself, either alone or through community and connection. Give yourself permission to be and do what feels right for you. Owning your struggles is the bridge to owning your healing.

Acknowledgments

I am still amazed and in awe that I've been granted the opportunity to write a book and share my words with the world. I am utterly grateful for the community of people in my life both online and offline who helped make this happen and supported me along the way. To my social media community, your endless support for my work is what has granted me the opportunity to bring this book to life, so I thank you for the role that you played in both the making and shaping of this book. I thank my parents for their love, their guidance, and investment in me from a young age to be the woman that I am today. I am grateful for my father's continued love and presence over me in spirit, and my mother's unconditional love, which has been nurturing and a source of peace in allowing me the space and time to write this book. To my family—you all make me honored to be the youngest of thirteen. I couldn't ask for a better group of older siblings. And to my family back home in Panama, I send my utmost gratitude and love for the ways you support me and celebrate me despite the distance. Uncle Ricky, although it deeply pains me that we are far away from each other, me on American soil and you in Panama, I want you to know that if you were here in front of me, I would tell you I love you. I wish I could hug you, and I thank you for being a second father to me.

I want to thank every single one of my friends who have lifted me up in love and support, have always seen greatness in me, have always cheered me on, and were always a source of encouragement when I forgot my purpose or lost sight of my potential. You all have played a vital role in helping me get to where I am today, and your endless encouragement does not go unnoticed, nor has it been taken for granted. Thank you, Nequa, for being my biggest cheerleader since we were six years old, and thank you, Shantia, for being a big sister and role model to me. I also want to thank my extended family and the community of people who have helped raise me and shape me into the woman that I am today.

To my agent, Laura Lee, I want to thank you for seeing potential in me and working with me on this project. You have helped me as a writer in so many ways, and I do not take that for granted. My team at TarcherPerigee, from day one, you have been the most wonderful and supportive team, and I am so glad and honored I had you all backing me up on this project.

I thank God for the wisdom He's given me, the guidance He has set before me, and the peace that He has been during all my storms, trials, and tribulations. I thank my ancestors, those who are known and those who aren't, for carving this path and lineage I've gotten to be a part of.

Last, I am proud of myself. I am proud of the little girl in me who had the courage to stop playing small and overcome her fears. I am proud of myself for taking chances, quitting, starting over, pivoting, and fighting hard as hell to give myself the life I felt I deserve. I am thankful for the woman I am, and for my community who helped me be the woman I am today. Thank you all!

Notes

1

THE STRUGGLE FOR WHOLENESS

9 **It shapes how we perceive the world:** Christine A. Padesky, "Schema Change Processes in Cognitive Therapy," *Clinical Psychology and Psychotherapy* 1, no. 5 (1994), 267–278.

10 **what it means to build healthy attachments:** Corinne Rees, "Childhood Attachment," *British Journal of General Practice* 57, no. 544 (2007): 920–922.

11 **the impact that sibling rivalry also has on young children:** Darlene Lancer, "Sibling Bullying and Abuse: The Hidden Epidemic," *Psychology Today*, February 3, 2020, https://www.psychologytoday.com/us/blog/toxic-relationships/202002/sibling-bullying-and-abuse-the-hidden-epidemic.

13 **they may dissociate as a survival tactic:** Dr. Shoshanah Lyons, *Dissociation in Children and Teens*, 2020, beaconhouse.org.uk.

13 **an out-of-body experience:** K. R. Choi, J. S. Seng, E. C. Briggs-King, et al., "Dissociation and PTSD: What Parents Should Know," 2018, https://www.nctsn.org/sites/default/files/resources/fact-sheet/data_at_a_glance_dissociation_and_ptsd_parents.pdf.

15 **Adverse Childhood Experiences:** Centers for Disease Control and Prevention and Kaiser Permanente, "Original ACE Questionnaire," Trauma-Informed Care, July 2019, https://www.traumainformedcare.chcs.org/resource/original-ace-questionnaire/.

15 **the Philadelphia ACE Survey:** "Philadelphia ACE Survey," Philadelphia ACE Project, n.d., https:// www.philadelphiaaces.org/philadelphia-ace-survey.

16 **three common reasons why young teens run away:** Lisa Davis, "Why Youth Run Away—National Runaway Prevention Month," Family Resources, November 26, 2019, https://familyresourcesinc.org/2019/11/why-youth-run-away/.

21 **the autonomic nervous system:** "Parasympathetic Nervous System (PSNS)," Cleveland Clinic, n.d., https://my.clevelandclinic.org/health/body/23266-parasympathetic-nervous-system-psns.

21 **which is a part of the body:** Joshua A. Waxenbaum, Vamsi Reddy, and Matthew Varacallo, "Anatomy, Autonomic Nervous System," National Library of Medicine, July 25, 2022, https://www.ncbi.nlm.nih.gov/books/NBK539845/.

24 **the ABC model:** Kirsten Nunez, "What Is the ABC Model in Cognitive Behavioral Therapy?," Healthline, April 17, 2020, https://www.healthline.com/health/abc-model.

2
THE STRUGGLE FOR HEALING

44 **form of complex trauma:** "What Is Child Trauma?," National Child Traumatic Stress Network, n.d., https:// www.nctsn.org/what-is-child-trauma/trauma-types/complex-trauma.

46 **cost society more than $458 billion:** Michele W. Berger, "Childhood Exposure to Trauma Costs Society $458 Billion Annually," November 6, 2019, https://penntoday.upenn.edu/news/childhood-exposure-trauma-costs-society-458-billion-annually.

53 **data to support a variety of core emotions:** Deborah Halber, "The Anatomy of Emotions," BrainFacts, September 6, 2018, https://www.brainfacts.org/thinking-sensing-and-behaving/emotions-stress-and-anxiety/2018/the-anatomy-of-emotions-090618.

60 **goal of distress tolerance:** Matthew Tull, "What Is Distress Tolerance?," Verywell Mind, July 17, 2020, https://www.verywellmind.com/distress-tolerance-2797294.

3
THE STRUGGLE FOR SAFE SPACES

74 *Girlhood Interrupted*: Rebecca Epstein, Jamilia J. Blake, and Thalia González, *Girlhood Interrupted: The Erasure of Black Girls' Childhood*, Georgetown Law Center on Poverty and Inequality Initiative on Gender Justice and Opportunity, n.d., https://genderjusticeandopportunity.georgetown.edu/wp-content/uploads/2020/06/girlhood-interrupted.pdf.

82 **internalized oppression:** "Healing from the Effects of Internalized Oppression," Community Tool Box, n.d., https://ctb.ku.edu/en/table-of-contents/culture/cultural-competence/healing-from-interalized-oppression/main.

84 **the World Trade Health Center Registry:** *World Trade Health Center Registry*, 2019, https:// www1.nyc.gov/assets/911health/downloads/pdf/registry/wtchr-annual-report2019.pdf.

95 **types of intimacy:** Acamea Deadwiler, "The 5 Types of Intimacy That Exist + How to Build Them in a Relationship," mindbodygreen, September 30, 2022, https://www.mindbodygreen.com/articles/types-of-intimacy-besides-sex.

96 **At the root of counterdependency:** Gregg Henriques, "Signs of Counter-Dependency: When Fear of Intimacy Is a Driving Force," *Psychology Today*, April 11, 2014, https://www.psychologytoday.com/us/blog/theory-knowledge/201404/signs-counter-dependency.

101 **forced sterilization among BIPOC:** Alexandra Stern, "Forced Sterilization Policies in the US Targeted Minorities and Those with Disabilities—and Lasted into the 21st Century," University of Michigan Institute for Healthcare Policy & Innovation, September 23, 2020, https://ihpi.umich.edu/news/forced-sterilization-policies-us-targeted-minorities-and-those-disabilities-and-lasted-21st.

101 **eugenics:** "Eugenics," History.com, October 28, 2019, https://www.history.com/topics/germany/eugenics.

101 **86 percent white clinicians:** Luona Lin, Karen Stamm, and Peggy Christidis, "How Diverse Is the Psychology Workforce?" American Psychological Association, 2018, https://www.apa.org/monitor/2018/02/datapoint.

4

THE STRUGGLE FOR UNCONDITIONAL LOVE

109 **backbone of society is the family unit:** Ashley Brown, "What Is the Importance of Family in Modern Society?" BetterHelp, September 30, 2022, https://www.betterhelp.com/advice/family/what-is-the-importance-of-family-in-modern-society/.

112 **Childhood trauma can impact an individual:** M. D. De Bellis and A. Zisk, "The Biological Effects of Childhood Trauma," *Child and Adolescent Psychiatric Clinics of North America* 23, no. 2 (April 2014): 185–222, https://doi.org/10.1016/j.chc.2014.01.002.

112 **Dysfunctional families can manifest as:** "Understanding Dysfunctional Relationship Patterns in Your Family," Brown University. n.d., https://www.brown.edu/campus-life/support/counseling-and-psychological-services/dysfunctional-family-relationships.

118 **theory of attachment:** Dr. Saul McLeod, "Bowlby's Attachment Theory," Simply-Psychology, 2017, https://www.simplypsychology.org/bowlby.html.

118 **four now well-known attachment styles:** Kendra Cherry, "The Different Types of Attachment Styles," Verywell Mind, May 26, 2022, https://www.verywellmind.com/attachment-styles-2795344.

119 **maternal deprivation hypothesis:** "Bowlby's Theory of Maternal Deprivation," Tutor2u, September 6, 2022, https://www.tutor2u.net/psychology/reference/bowlbys-theory-of-maternal-deprivation.

120 **an adult child who yearns for closeness and connection:** Regina Sullivan and Elizabeth Norton Lasley, "Fear in Love: Attachment, Abuse, and the Developing Brain," *Cerebrum*, September 1, 2010, https://www.ncbi.nlm.nih.gov/pmc/articles/PMC3574772/.

139 **Termination of a parent-child relationship:** Dr. Lucy Blake, *Hidden Voices: Family Estrangement in Adulthood*, StandAlone, n.d., https://www.standalone.org.uk/wp-content/uploads/2015/12/HiddenVoices.FinalReport.pdf.

5

THE STRUGGLE FOR INTIMACY

152 **people who frequently use dating apps report higher levels:** Emily R. Wilhite and Kim Fromme, "Swiping Right: Alcohol, Online Dating, and Sexual Hookups in Postcollege Women," *Psychology of Addictive Behaviors* 33, no. 6 (2019): 552–560, https://doi.org/10.1037/adb0000493.

168 **The divorce rate increased 21 percent:** Maddy Savage, "Why the Pandemic Is Causing Spikes in Break-ups and Divorces," BBC, December 6, 2020, https://www.bbc.com/worklife/article/20201203-why-the-pandemic-is-causing-spikes-in-break-ups-and-divorces.

179 **Loneliness as an epidemic:** Roge Karma, "Former Surgeon General Vivek Murthy on America's Loneliness Epidemic: Why Americans Are So Lonely—and What We Can Do About It," Vox, May 11, 2020, https://www.vox.com/2020/5/11/21245087/america-loneliness-epidemic-coronavirus-pandemic-together.

6

THE STRUGGLE FOR FULFILLMENT

198 **forty-seven million people quit their jobs:** Stephanie Ferguson, "Understanding America's Labor Shortage: The Most Impacted Industries," US Chamber of Commerce, September 7, 2022, https://www.uschamber.com/workforce/understanding-americas-labor-shortage-the-most-impacted-industries.

198 **Black and Hispanic workers had a much harder time:** Megan Cassella, "Black Workers, Hammered by Pandemic, Now Being Left Behind in Recovery," Politico, March 3, 2021, https://www.politico.com/news/2021/03/23/black-workers-pandemic-recovery-477640.

199 **the CROWN Act:** The CROWN Act, n.d., https://www.thecrownact.com.

217 **seven different types of rest:** Saundra Dalton-Smith, "The 7 Types of Rest That Every Person Needs," Ideas.Ted, January 6, 2021, https://ideas.ted.com/the-7-types-of-rest-that-every-person-needs/.

218 **calming those neurons in the brain:** "Sleep, Learning, and Memory," Division of Sleep Medicine at Harvard Medical School, 2017, https://healthysleep.med.harvard.edu/healthy/matters/benefits-of-sleep/learning-memory.

7

THE STRUGGLE OF BEING HUMAN

242 **Meditation and deep-breathing exercises are great:** Paige Fowler, "Breathing Techniques for Stress Relief," WebMD, January 17, 2022, https://www.webmd.com/balance/stress-management/stress-relief-breathing-techniques.

245 **Grounding techniques are practices beneficial for cultivating mindfulness:** Kirsten Weir, 2020. "Nurtured by Nature," American Psychological Association, April 1, 2020, https://www.apa.org/monitor/2020/04/nurtured-nature.

251 **dopamine, serotonin, endorphins, and oxytocin:** Crystal Raypole, "How to Hack Your Hormones for a Better Mood," Healthline, July 26, 2022, https://www.healthline.com/health/happy-hormone.

Index

Index

  manifestations of, 112–13
  and maternal deprivation hypothesis, 119–20
  minimizing contact in, 133
  and the mother wound, 116–22
  and parents' inability to love/care for children, 117
  privacy violations in, 133
  and Relational Building Plans, 144–46
  terminating difficult relationships in, 133–34
  values clashing in, 133–34
  violence in, 111, 135

education, withholding of, 136
emotions
  awareness of, 30–31
  building maturity, 65–66
  and childhood trauma, 17
  of children in dysfunctional families, 14–15
  emotional blackmail, 138
  emotional boundaries, 28, 29
  emotional immaturity, 134–39, 162–63
  emotional intimacy, 95
  emotional rest, 223–26
  health practices for dealing with distress, 59–60
  identifying, 65
  immature behaviors, 61–63
  myth of good/bad, 53–54
  naming, 21–22
  parents' criticisms of, 135
  regulation of, 58–60
  storytelling aspect of, 54
  suppressing negative, 53, 54, 56
  and tolerance for distress, 58–61
employment and work environments
  advancement opportunities in, 198–99
  and the American Dream, 199–201
  and burnout culture, 197–98, 224
  discriminatory practices in, 199
  and the Great Resignation, 198
  and myth of work-life balance, 214–15
  as related to worth/value, 211
endorphins, 22, 251–52
enmeshment, 113
entitlement, 203

envy, 189
escapism, healthy, 60, 103
executive functioning skills, 217, 218
exercise, 218
expectations, adjusting, 174
experiential intimacy, 95

families
  family units, 109–10
  internalized oppression rooted in family ideologies, 89–91
  traditions in, 32
  See also dysfunctional families
faultiness, feelings of, 1
fear, living despite, 78–80. *See also* anxiety
feminism, white, 77
A Field Guide to Getting Lost (Solnit), 209
fifty-fifty myth in relationships, 172–73
fight, flight, or freeze, 21, 59, 112, 245
financial insecurity/abuse, 136
fitting in, 4
5-4-3-2-1 Method (grounding practice), 245
flexibility in friendships, 192–93
Floyd, George, 76
food
  of BIPOC cultures, 104–5
  bonding over, 223
  food apartheid, 44
forgetfulness, chronic, 13
forgiveness, 35–38
friendships
  avoidance of closeness in, 187
  being the problematic friend, 188–94
  boundaries in, 190–91, 192
  breakups in, 185–86, 187–88
  and combating loneliness, 180
  and community-care, 194
  and co-regulation, 178–79
  exhausting, 226
  and healing work, 153
  importance of, 186–88
  levels/types of, 181, 182–86
  and need for connection, 194
  needs in, 186
  practicing self-attunement in, 176, 177–78

- 266 -

Index

suicide ideation, 15
sympathetic nervous system, 21, 245

tantrums, adult, 19, 63
television shows, rewatching, 22–23
therapy, 41–42, 99–102, 104, 141
third wheel, feeling like a, 179
Three Good Things gratitude practice, 248
time boundaries, 28, 29–30
The Tinder Swindler (Netflix series), 151
touch deprivation, 179
toxic positivity, 52–57
trauma
    and ACEs questionnaire, 15–17, 44, 110–11
    complex, 45
    costs of unhealed, 46
    impact on brain development in children,
        15–17
    and inner-child healing, 18–20
    intergenerational, 84–87, 98–99
    manifestations of, 44–45
    memory loss related to, 13
    message of staying small, 208
    and nervous system, 20–21, 22–23
    of people formerly enslaved, 85–86
    and radical acceptance, 130–32
    releasing, with body scans, 244
    of September 11, 2001, terrorist attacks,
        84–85
    snowball effect of, 46
    stored in the body, 84–85
    types of, 45
triggers
    and ABC model of boundaries, 25, 26
    and grounding practices, 245
    and journaling, 248
    and Relational Building Plans, 144–45
    responding to, 38
    and setting boundaries in families, 128–30
trust
    lack of trust in others, 96
    in oneself, 252–53
truth, denying one's, 50–51
Tubman, Harriet, 80

unfairness, feelings of, 51

unloveable, feelings of being, 33
urgency culture, 213, 223
US Chamber of Commerce, 198

values, defining, 32–35
victim mode, 131
violence
    in community, 17
    domestic, 136
    impact on children, 15, 16, 46, 110–11
    in parent-child relationships, 111, 135
    race-based, 77
    trauma associated with, 44
visualization exercises, 243
vulnerability
    and acquaintances, 183
    and combating loneliness, 180
    and counterdependency, 96–97
    and friendships, 181
    and healing from dysfunctional families,
        114–15
    and judgmental people, 28
    and personal strength, 94
    required for mental strength and change, 7–8

wanting more for oneself, 49–50
white gaze, 81–83
white supremacy, 76–77, 78
withdrawal, 51
women
    avoiding leadership roles, 87
    and gender oppression, 45
    and gender roles, 90–91
    and imposter syndrome, 87–88
    strong black woman trope, 92–99, 100
wonder and play, sense of, 221–22
work-life balance, myth of, 214–15
worthlessness, sense of, 33
writing, 59–60, 219

yoga, 218
Yousafzai, Malala, 80

Zoom fatigue, 228

About the Author

Minaa B. is a writer, author, and the founder of Minaa B. Consulting, a mental health consulting practice that works with organizations to help them develop psychological safety and become mental health inclusive. She is also a licensed mental health professional and worked as a therapist specializing in treating depression, anxiety, and trauma. Minaa earned her master's degree in social work from New York University. Her work is rooted in teaching people how to cultivate self-care and self-advocacy through boundaries and community-care.

An expert in her field, Minaa has been featured in a variety of media outlets, such as *Red Table Talk*, *Peace of Mind with Taraji*, *Today*, the BBC, *Essence*, and more. Minaa is a contributing writer for Well+Good and sits on the Mental Health Advisory Committee for Wondermind, a mental fitness company co-founded by Selena Gomez. Minaa runs a popular mental health account where she teaches and provides tools to help people manage their mental health. Minaa lives in New York City, and you can learn more about her by visiting www.minaab.com.